Dody Johnson 5/15/12

from my heart
to yours ♥

Fugue (fy$\overline{oo}$g): A period of amnesia during which the affected person seems to be conscious and make rational decisions, but, upon recovery, the period is not remembered.

Fugue

I Can't Remember
How I Got Here . . .

A Memoir

Dody Johnson

North Star Press of St. Cloud, Inc.
St. Cloud, Minnesota

Cover Design by John Thornberg

First Edition: August 2011

Printed in the United States of America

Published by
North Star Press of St. Cloud, Inc.
P.O. Box 451
St. Cloud, Minnesota 56302

northstarpress.com

To Sarah Johannah Holbrook

Sometimes it feels like you and me
against the world —Helen Reddy

Acknowledgments

I thank my friend Lynn LeFeber and my fellow writers from River Voices: Tracy Gulliver, Todd Gulliver, John Thornberg, Suzanne Cecere, Beth Hagert, Mary Lynn Regnier, Peter Schwarz, and Moose for their unwavering support. They constantly encouraged me to dig deeper into my past. Without your relentless help, I would not have finished the book.

Special thanks to my husband, Lyle, who supported me unconditionally, making it possible for me to write.

Thanks to Patricia Weaver Francisco, my mentor, for your help in preparing this book for publication. Working with Patricia was made possible by a grant from the East Central Regional Development Commission and the East Central Arts Council with funds provided by the McKnight Foundation.

I have changed the names of people in my memoir who are not my immediate family to protect their privacy.

Table of Contents

1

Silenced

I LIVED MY LIFE AS SILENTLY AS I COULD. I spoke my first words when I was five and they were to my beautiful kindergarten teacher. It wasn't safe to talk at home. My siblings and I never knew what was going to make our parents angry so we tried to be as quiet as possible. Out of sight was good and out of the house was better. During my teenage years I often reflected on my childhood, trying to figure out why I was so fearful of people and why I was confused and disoriented most of the time. I never thought my childhood was perfect, but I didn't think it was that different from my friends. My parent's fought a lot, drank too much and inflicted corporal punishment on their children. What household didn't? I thought we were a pretty normal family. So why did I feel so pathetic?

I actually grew up with little memory of growing up. Disappearing was how I lived my life, only I didn't know I was disappearing. I wasn't aware of the severity of the verbal and physical abuse in our home, and never fathomed the sexual abuse until my childhood memories surfaced later in life.

I left my parents home on my eighteenth birthday and moved frequently across the country trying to find a comfortable place. I married five times and asked one of my husbands once,

"Why did you let me beat on you?" He said, "All that anger came from somewhere. I knew you must have been hurt terribly in your past and I wanted you to get it out." My poor husbands and daughter witnessed my violent screaming episodes. I would pick up furniture and throw it across the room, smashing it into pieces. I needed to hurt something. My pain was bigger than me and I tried to scream myself off of this planet. Sometimes I remembered the rage and my destructive behavior. Sometimes I didn't.

I've always had memory of wanting to die as a child but never knew why. I carried my suicidal thoughts into my adult life by flirting with death as I sped down rolling, flexuous country roads. I picked up hitch-hikers that looked like Charles Manson thinking *maybe this will be my last day*. At the supermarket where I worked, I stood close to the incinerator leaving my arm inside the fires and wanting to jump in.

At the age of forty-five my first repressed memory surfaced and life as I knew it was no longer. My past as I remembered it didn't exist. My story is about growing up in a violent home where my parents raised us with verbal, physical and sexual abuse. I would not have survived without my older brother, Artie. He and I talked in secret for years about how wonderful life was going to be when we moved out.

My dreams of leaving home helped me until I left. Growing up in my environment prepared me to live my life in a state of confusion that I tried to keep a secret. I never found home no matter how many times I moved and I never found someone to love me no matter how many times I married until one day I heard a voice from my past and I listened.

2

A Day at the Beach

M Y FIRST LOVE AFFAIR IS THE ONE I'm still in. It's with the ocean. I love the ocean. She speaks to me and I speak back. I love how she looks and I love all of her emotions. She understands my deepest feelings. Sometimes she's wild with loud, crashing waves towering over me, and sometimes she's mild and gentle, tickling my toes. I sink into the wet sand and she massages my feet as she swirls around me.

Sometimes she appears to be holding all the world's tears. She feels so much pain that she has to scream her anger thrashing to shore. There are times I need to sit close and cry with her.

There are times when the ocean is my best playmate. I run out to her and she catches me and takes me up high and I ride with her as she quickly lowers me to the sand. Then there are times I love to stand in the water knee deep and watch her build, settle, and then build some more. Like she's teasing me and then all of a sudden she's ready to let go and I try so very hard not to let her knock me down as she presses hard against my body. Sometimes I collapse and she wins. Sometimes I'm an unmovable pillar of steel and I win. Sometimes I let her chase me as I run away from her. And, sometimes she catches me.

This love affair with the ocean started when I was a child. My father introduced me to her. Once a year in August, early in the morning, and still dark outside, he would go around the house waking up my siblings and me. We made up five in all. Kathy, the oldest was the serious one, well beyond her years. She acted like a little, bossy mother, but we knew she loved us. Next, came Artie, the clown in the family who turned everything into fun. When I think of Artie, I see his wide smile. As the second daughter, middle child, I had the best of both worlds. I was loved and cared for by my two older siblings and loved and revered by my two younger ones. I couldn't lose. Bill and Bob arrived last. We always lumped them together because you rarely saw a Bill without a Bob.

We were trying to wake up at that ungodly hour, bumping into each other as we rushed to the bathroom to be first in line. We started dressing, putting our clothes on over our bathing suits. Next, we helped by taking loads of stuff to the car. I was still tired as we drove away from our house in the dark. Our neighborhood looked different without movement in it. Order and quiet replaced the delivery trucks and kids yelling to each other from too far away. It felt strange to be the only family awake and the only car on the road while everyone else was still sleeping. I used to pretend we were escaping out of the city to freedom. I loved looking out the car window at the quiet scenery. I knew I was seeing things my friends had never seen. One has to get up very early to see a city still sleeping.

We arrived at Jones Beach in the dark, and started the many trips from the car to our spot near the ocean. My eyes adjusted to the darkness and eventually I could see where sky touched water. Being as close as we were to New York City, our sky was always black. The first time I ever saw stars was during the big blackout in November of 1965. I stayed up all night in our front yard looking at all the bright little lights above me. It was the most spectacular sight I ever witnessed. I had no idea that some people saw this all the time.

My father started setting up the grill as we arranged all the coolers near by. Besides providing food, shelter, and clothing for the family, his big contribution was creating childhood memories. My father was a romantic, and an artist. He earned his money in the corporate world, climbing that ladder of success, and I believe he did well in the business world because he applied that same imagination and motivation he shared with us, to his peers. As he put the bacon and sausage on, my siblings and I spread out all the blankets on the sand. We would arrange our toys in the designated toy area. We had beach balls to play with, shovels and pails to build sandcastles, flipper fins so we could swim like the sharks and inner tubes so my little brothers wouldn't drown. Artie always brought his box of army men, and Kathy was never without her transistor radio. I can still remember when "Yellow Polka Dot Bikini" came on. Some day I was going to have a yellow polka dot bikini.

My dad always timed the breakfast just right. When he finished cooking, I understood why he was on such a regimented time schedule. He wanted us all to have our plates in front of us just as the "Sun" started to peek above the horizon. For me, this was my first experience with Dinner Theatre, only it was Breakfast Theatre. We all sat there, eating our breakfast in awe, watching the sun perform in front of us. The colors were breathtaking as her beaming round face peeped over the edge of the world as if to see who was watching. The ocean, sand, and sky were her stage, and when she made her full appearance, my family and I screamed excitedly and applauded as loudly as we could. It would be another year before we saw this play again. It always amazed me that we were the only ones on the beach. I found it hard to understand why no one else wanted to see the show.

By the time we finished eating and cleaning up the pots and pans, it was time to take off our sweatshirts. Slowly, families started arriving until a steady stream paraded from the parking lot to the beach, and all of a sudden a clear spot was hard to find. I heard laughter, yelling and little girls' high-pitched screams as the cold water hit against their bodies for the first time.

Next, the dreaded scream, I hated this scream, and we could count on hearing it every time we went to the beach. It was the scream that came after the jellyfish stung my mother. I am proud to say nothing in the ocean has ever stung or bitten me. I guess because we are so close and she knows how to protect me. My mother on the other hand had a different relationship with the ocean. She could not stand at water's edge without something grabbing onto her. Maybe her fear of water and not being able to swim attracted them. Well, anyway I always felt sad for her because she had to leave her nice time and have the jellyfish replaced with screaming, crying and pain. After it was removed from her foot, she retreated to her blanket and stayed there until we were ready to load the car to go home. She had to wait a very long time because we still had lunch and dinner to eat.

When we went on family outings, most often my mother ended up angry and by herself. My father decided to ignore her, not wanting to get dragged into a fight. And, because she was being ignored, her rage would build until she left us. Her body was still on the blanket, but there was no one home when you looked into her eyes. I never knew where my mother went, and I had mixed feelings about her leaving us. I felt sad that she had to leave earth, but I was glad that she wasn't screaming at the top of her lungs. It was embarrassing and scary when she vented her rage. We knew when we went out in public something was going to happen to her. We just didn't know what or how. So, we spent our day playing and exploring at the beach and trying very hard not to let mother dampen our spirits or ruin our fun.

At dusk, Dad prepared the grill for cooking again. He always fixed steaks, corn on the cob, and potato salad for dinner. We ate until the noisy sun disappeared and the quiet moon lit the sky. After dinner, we all went for a long walk, except Mom, who still couldn't leave her blanket. The grill needed time to cool down before loading it back into the car, so a walk was a good idea. We laughed and talked about our day. We told about the people we met and the fun we had. We always named our best part and our worst part of the day. We all knew what Mom's worst part of the day was, and then we started talking about the jellyfish, and making jokes about why the jellyfish liked Mom the best.

Cleaning up after eighteen hours at the beach was a project and a half. There was so much to throw out and organize and carry to the car. Dad orchestrated the tearing down of our compound just as he did the building of it. We acquired new piles. The garbage pile was next to the rock pile, which we collected on the beach for my dad's rock gardens at home. We had the shell pile next to the wet towel pile. "Kathy and Dody, shake out all the blankets. Artie, start taking this stuff to the car. I'll load it when I get there. Dody, watch your little brothers," my dad directed.

It was like magic when we took that last load to the car. I looked everywhere across the beach and not a soul was to be found. It was dark and empty just like when we arrived.

I took one last look at my best friend. She was calm now. Small white-tipped waves gently rolling to shore as she also came in for the night. I thanked her for helping me through that day of fun and devastation. I felt drawn to her and sad to leave. Who will help me when my mother disappears tomorrow?

Whenever I feel too much of the world's craziness, I go and visit my lover. She still encourages me to go on.

3

A Six-Year-Old Business

OW DO YOU TEACH A PINT-SIZE six-year-old girl to provide for the family? You fill her red wagon with tins of butter-cream candies and tell her not to come home until they're all sold. While my father climbed the corporate ladder to his success, he explained the basics of work to me.

"Dody, you'll never lack for food or a roof over your head if you learn the skills to sell. When you're an adult, you may find yourself between jobs, and if you can sell, you'll never have to worry about paying the bills. You will be compensated for your hard work."

I had no idea what my father was talking about and it didn't matter. On Saturday mornings during the summer, Artie, my older brother, and I stood in the garage while Dad filled my red wagon and Artie's canvas bag with tins of candy.

"Dad, that's a lot of candy to sell. I won't be home until dark," my small voice let out.

"If you sell it all today, you can play tomorrow. But remember, you will sell tomorrow what you don't sell today."

Dad yelled to me as I walked down the sidewalk pulling my inventory behind me, "Make me proud."

We always had to sell to new people, so each time I went out I ventured farther from home. Dad was a stickler about not selling to people we knew.

"You'll never learn powerful selling skills by taking money from friends and family. The best way to learn is cold calling, door to door with strangers."

Every step I took towards the front door of an unfamiliar home was filled with trepidation. Who would open the door? The moms were my favorite. They were nice and often bought a tin or two. The dads were okay sometimes, and sometimes they slammed the door in my face. I hated when that happened and I had to muster all the strength inside me to keep on going. The kids were the worst. They answered the door and then didn't tell anyone I was there, so I waited and waited. Do I ring the bell again or do I walk away? I had too much candy to sell, so I rang the bell again.

In 1959 it was perfectly normal for a six-year-old girl to wander around the neighborhood knocking on strangers' doors. We didn't get paid for selling because as Dad put it, "You two are lucky. Most people have to pay a hefty fee to receive good sales training."

The money we earned paid for the candy and the profit went towards the household expenses. I can still hear my father say, "You enjoy the food prepared for you, don't you? The clothes you wear are lovely, and I'm sure you appreciate having a warm house to live in."

Artie and I went in opposite directions to sell our candy and came home each Saturday, late in the afternoon with an empty wagon and canvas bag. We had two motivators to get the job done in one day. First motivator was, Artie and I raced to finish the task and turned it into a contest. The winner was the first one home with all goods sold. Artie always won, but he was three years older than me and more experienced. The second motivator was not having to sell the next day.

During the week, when we finished our chores, Artie and I pulled my wagon around the neighborhood looking for treasures in the street to sell. It was fun peddling our own inventory. Our biggest seller was broken colored glass. We sold each piece for five cents. We sold bottle caps for a penny, necklaces and bracelets for a dime, and sometimes we even found money. Our selling approach was a little different from my father's. We sold only to people we knew. When we ran out of unique items to sell, we sold lemonade on the front sidewalk. The same stand we used to sell lemonade was also Artie's comic book stand. He sold his old, worn comic books and traded some for books he hadn't read yet. I was his comic book assistant.

I totally understood this work thing after my first summer on the job. I worked hard and sometimes I liked it, sometimes I didn't. The best part was being rewarded for my hard work. Once a week Artie and I rode our bikes to the candy store with the money earned from selling our treasures found in the street. We purchased whatever our hearts desired. I guess you could say I was well compensated.

4

George and Gracie

MY PARENTS WERE SOCIAL JUNKIES. Actually, "social" doesn't even begin to describe them. They were real performers, the kind of talent you would see on Ed Sullivan. Ed would have booked them in a heartbeat. They were right up there with George and Gracie. Dad was charismatic, an on the edge-of-your-seat storyteller. Mom would bring people to their knees gasping for air with her quick wit and antics.

I loved the entertaining part of them that went out into the world. We were safe when people were present. I loved hearing the sound of my father's voice when he told a story. One minute he was full of thunder and the next barely a whisper. Needless to say, he had everyone's attention. Just like Gracie, Mom told stories about her day and acted them out like she was playing charades. She was always on stage when her friends were nearby.

One evening after dinner the neighborhood was in our backyard. The adults were enjoying after-dinner cocktails and the children feeding peanuts to the squirrels. Mom stood before everyone telling her story about the cop giving her a ticket that day for not returning her cart to the supermarket. That was before cart corrals.

"I can't even run a simple errand to the grocery store without the Shopping Cart Patrol stopping me. After loading the groceries into the car, I push the cart away and slid into the driver seat. As I start to back out of my parking space, I'm surprised by a tap, tap on my window. Leaning down is a snot-nosed kid in a cop uniform."

"Ma'am, did you see who last used this cart?"

"I did officer, is there a problem?"

"Yes, I have to ticket you for not returning it to the store."

"Are you sure you have to do that? I promise I will never, not return my cart again, and I will return this one right now."

"Sorry ma'am, I have to ticket you," and he points to this huge sign, 'RETURN YOUR CART TO THE STORE. THIS IS ENFORCED AND VIOLATORS WILL BE PROSECUTED.' "It would be unfair to ticket others and not you."

"I won't tell if you don't. He hands me the ticket with a dirty look. So now I have to appear in court because I didn't return my shopping cart to the store." Everyone is laughing and enjoying her antics.

Mom didn't tell her friends how angry she was as we drove away, "What a stupid law. He's so almighty and powerful giving tickets to women in supermarket parking lots." Once we were home we all disappeared, not knowing where Mom's anger would take her. She was already screaming and throwing things, and we didn't want to be in the path of her fury. Mom never did well when someone had power to make her do something she didn't want to do.

I wished Mom and Dad could be funny all the time, but when their audience was gone, so went their charming person-alities. Mom never acted out in front of her adoring public the way she screamed at us, or threw away our toys. She never demon-strated how she stayed in bed for days with her door closed. Dad didn't tell the story about coming home from work and pouring himself a Scotch and then another, and another, or about passing out in his chair every night. They've never told the story about how some evenings there was more food on the kitchen ceiling than on our dinner plates. As good as Mom and Dad appeared to the world outside, inside behind closed doors they were dangerous to each other and to us. I wished we could always be outside where it was safe.

I wanted my parents to like me and I tried to do things right. I wanted to know why they couldn't be nice to me like they were to their friends. Well, Dad seemed to like me okay, sometimes, but I was pretty sure Mom didn't like me at all. Five kids were just too many to deal with. The burden of caring for us and keeping up with Dad's career, her house, and the yard was downright oppressive.

To the outside world we appeared to be the All-American Family with Mom in charge of the house and Dad in charge of the yard. Sunday afternoon's Artie and I would weed, cut the grass, sweep the driveway and do whatever else needed to be done. Dad took charge from inside, recovering from his hangover, or having a beer with the neighbors.

While Kathy took care of Billy and Bobby, I cleaned and did the ironing. I was six when Mom brought out the ironing board and taught me how to iron my dad's shirts properly. She said to me, "Since he likes you so much, you can do his ironing." Why was I being punished because my dad liked me?

Artie was in charge of straightening up the house. He vacuumed and made sure books, magazines, games and all the other clutter were put away in their proper places. In our need for Mom and Dad to love us, we did the best we could to help lighten their heavy load. And, every Saturday night they were rewarded for their hard work. They had a party to go to.

All the grown-ups in the neighborhood took turns giving the Saturday night party, and you couldn't have a party without Art and Marilyn. They were the party. Just like teenagers, they lived for Saturday night. When I was between the ages of five and eight, I remember my parents leaving on Saturday evenings. This was "Happy Time" for Artie and me. That's what we called it, "Happy Time." We ate TV dinners in front of the television and watched movies. Kathy was always doing something responsible, like feeding the younger boys, bathing them and putting them to bed. After the boys fell asleep, she retired to her room and read.

Artie and I loved it when Mom and Dad went out, but it was bittersweet, because we knew they would return. We had to make the most of our Happy Time. No matter how hard we laughed, we knew it would end. Just being able to laugh was a rich commodity. We always hoped that the next time they came home it would be different.

Eventually, we'd go to bed, but we didn't sleep, because we knew our Happy Time would be replaced with fear and pain. Once I was under my covers, Artie would appear in my doorway, and slowly move out of sight as if he were disappearing into the wall. I always laughed when he did that.

"Artie, I wish we could disappear. Isn't there someplace we can go?"

"Someday, we won't live here anymore and life will be wonderful. It'll be just how we want it to be."

I hear noise at the front door as my father tries to unlock it. They are drunk and yelling at each other. I'm scared and I hurt inside. My body tightens. I can't swallow, barely breathing. My father yells Artie's name and then mine. Kathy is always standing next to my mother when we get there. My father orders my brother to remove his shirt, and in his drunken stupor, beats him with his belt at the bottom of the stairs. In his graveled voice, he yells what a worthless piece of shit Artie is, and that no one will ever want to hire him. He'll be a bum all his life. He'll live on the streets with his bum friends. I can't watch. I close my eyes. I cry. I want to do something. I want to kill Dad. I hate Mom for just standing there and not doing anything. The skin on his back is turning red from the belt. My brother makes no sound, shows no emotion, and just holds on tight to the railing so he won't fall. I want to die. My dad yells at me to watch because this is what will happen to me if I misbehave.

I never knew why we had to go through this weekly ritual when my parents staggered home. And, I never figured out what they thought Artie had done to misbehave. I was with him all evening and he was nothing but a good brother and a son to be proud of. All we did was watch TV and laugh.

5

Fantasyland

IMAGINATION AND PRETENDING FILLED my days with excitement and gave me pleasure and control of my world. My real life was full of fear and pain. My pretend world was beautiful. Any child would love to live the life I made up. When I wasn't with Artie, who made life fun and exciting, I pretended I was somewhere else and I pretended I was someone else. When we lived in Garden City, our neighbors, the Edward's, lived on one side of us and an old man and woman lived on the other side. Mr. Bell lived across the street and Mr. and Mrs. Knight lived a few houses down. Looking back to when I lived on Pell Terrace, I see them reaching out to me and trying to help. I'm sure they heard the fighting and screaming that came from our house, not to mention this strange little girl that walked around their neighborhood.

Mrs. Edwards often made me a snack in the afternoon. She filled a plate with either homemade cookies or a peanut butter and jelly sandwich always accompanied with a cold glass of milk. I liked being in her house sitting in the big comfy chair with a TV tray placed in front of me. We just sat and visited with each other. Sometimes after my snack she brought out crayons and a coloring book. One day my mother called for me and when she saw me walk out of the Edwards's house, I was forbidden to ever step foot in there again. I didn't understand what the crime was. I often ran into Mr. Bell when I was outside and we had long talks together. He loved to ask, "Dody, what are you thinking?"

"Nothing."

"That's not possible. The brain is always thinking something. What are you thinking this very moment?"

"Nothing. I'm really not thinking anything at all." I believed him and thought the brain was always thinking something, but I knew it wasn't safe to tell him what I was thinking.

Mrs. Knight was taller than any woman I ever saw and much taller than my dad. I thought it unusual to see a woman taller than men. Her husband traveled frequently to other countries for work and she often went with him. She asked my Mom if I could stay with her when Mr. Knight traveled without her because she was afraid to stay in the house alone. Mom said yes. So every time Mr. Knight went on a trip without his wife, I stayed with Mrs. Knight. It was fun and she showered me with lots of attention when I had sleepovers at her house. She and Mr. Knight had the biggest bed I ever saw. I thought they had it specially made because they were both so tall. At night time after we put on our pajamas, Mrs. Knight made a big bowl of buttered popcorn and we sat on her bed and watched movies. I loved staying with Mrs. Knight. Most people saw her as a polished, world traveler, serious woman. I felt privileged to see her fun side. She laughed and told me funny stories about her family because she knew how much I loved her stories. Mrs. Knight was always bringing me toys that belonged to her daughter when she was my age. Mom never let me keep any of them. She threw them out after Mrs. Knight left and said, "We don't take charity in this house." She never told her I couldn't have them, so the toys kept coming and Mom kept throwing them out.

Mrs. Knight always gave me a costume from the country she had just visited. I loved to wake up in the morning, pick out a country and write a story about a girl from that far away land. Next, I put on my costume and became that girl. When I was a Japanese girl, I covered my face with baby powder and put on my mother's red lipstick and out into the world went this little geisha. I walked up and down the sidewalk pretending I was from Japan and experiencing the neighborhood for the first time. The old man and woman next door stopped to say hello and welcome me to the United States and Garden City. They asked me so many questions, how long was I here for, how do I spend my days, where was I staying? But of course I couldn't answer them because I didn't know how to speak English. I shrugged my shoulders and looked confused when they talked.

During first, second and third grade I pretended a lot and acted out the stories I made up. I disappeared, blocking out fourth, fifth and sixth grade and have no memory of those years.

6

It's Not My Fault

I loved school until the third grade. I was as quiet as a mouse at home, but in school I laughed and played with the other kids. It didn't start out that way. My kindergarten teacher helped me not to be afraid and encouraged me to have fun, and I loved her. She was so kind and beautiful with long blond hair. She looked and spoke like an angel. She was always trying to get me to play games with the other kids. But, I didn't want to leave the safety of being near her and I loved it when she put her arms around me. Finally, with her persistence, I played. At first I was scared. I didn't want the kids to look at me and see how scared I was. But, it didn't take long before I loved the games. I even looked forward to being the Farmer, in the Farmer in the Dell. Everyday, I couldn't wait to go to school.

First grade was great! Miss Kirsch was my teacher and that was the year I learned to read and write. I loved reading stories and making up my own. I pretended Dick and Jane were Artie and me. We were all over the neighborhood chasing Spot. My books took me to so many new places, my world just got a lot bigger.

Second grade was the best! We created works of art. We made bowls from record albums by putting them in the oven. The edges curled from the heat and we painted them. I made the

19

traditional lumpy ashtray from clay. We made an airplane out of cardboard that we actually fit inside. Mrs. Flynn, our teacher would tell us all about the places to which we pretended to fly. We went on a field trip to Radio City Music Hall where I saw my first ballet. I gave serious thought to becoming a ballerina. What little girl didn't when she saw the beautiful dance? At school, I laughed and had a lot of friends. I was happy there, it was my safe place.

I remember the first day of school entering third grade. I was the first student to arrive. I usually was. I was a walker and left home as early as I could to enter this wonderful place. *"Wow, I love my new classroom."* A name was written on the chalkboard, *"Mr. Stewart, is that my teacher's name? Do I have a man for a teacher?"* I didn't know if I liked that. *"I hope he's nice like my other teachers."* Then I chose my desk, front row center. I sat down and looked up at the alphabet above the chalkboard. It displayed upper and lower case letters in cursive. I was so excited and couldn't wait to learn how to write like a grown-up. My excited anticipation for the third grade did not turn out as I had hoped.

It was during the third grade that I wanted to die for the first time. I believed there was a God and every day I would lie on my back on our front lawn and look up at the sky and talk to Him.

"God, it's too hard to be alive. I'm scared to go home and now I'm scared to go to school. Mr. Stewart touches me just like Dad does, but that's okay. It's worse when Dad's friends touch me. I don't know them and they're creepy. I hate Mr. Stewart. Why won't he let me do the school work with the other kids? The kids don't like me anymore. They won't play with me at recess. They laugh at me and call me names and teacher's pet and they make up songs about baby Dody."

I brought my report card home at the end of the school year and it showed I had failed the third grade. My teacher wrote a note to my parents saying I needed to redo the class again. My mother grabbed me by the arm, my feet barely touching the ground and off we went to school. We marched straight into my classroom and Mom waved the offending report card in Mr. Stewart's face.

"What in hell is this all about? Why am I just hearing about this now? All of Dody's other report cards were fine and now all of a sudden she has failed the year? What am I going to tell my husband? He won't believe this is the first I'm hearing about it, and he won't accept his daughter failing third grade." Mom turned to me. "Don't I always ask you if you have homework, and don't you always say no."

Mr. Stewart began, "Mrs. White, Dody is very shy, and I felt she needed time to come out of her shell. I didn't want to put too much pressure on her, so at the start of each day I would ask Dody what she would like to do, and I always gave her three choices. One, she could do the work with the rest of the class, two, she could go outside to the playground, or three, she could paint in the back of the classroom at the easel. When Dody chose the playground, I picked her up and cradled her like a baby singing Lull-A-Bye-Baby to her as I carried her to the swings."

"Are you F------ Crazy? Dody is here to learn, not make choices about painting or the playground. Dody, why didn't you tell me you weren't doing school work, and that your teacher was carrying you around like a baby? What am I going to tell your father?"

I knew it wasn't my report card she was upset about, it was hers. She had failed at being a mom and here was the proof. I kept quiet. I didn't tell anyone that it wasn't the way Mr. Stewart said it was. I was never given any choices. All I wanted to do was the classwork with the rest of the kids, but I NEVER had that opportunity. Mr. Stewart carried me out to the swings if it wasn't raining or too cold and I sat by myself with tears rolling down my face, wishing I could be inside learning the school work with my friends. When the weather was bad, I painted at the easel in the back of the classroom.

My mother grabbed my arm and marched us down to the principal's office. Mrs. Flynn, my second grade teacher was also the school principal. Mom told her what Mr. Stewart had been doing all year.

"Mrs. Flynn, I can't believe you weren't aware of this. I know you wouldn't have allowed it." Mrs. Flynn's face turned red and her mouth wide open, but no words came out. "Didn't anybody think it was strange that Dody was on the playground during the school day? Didn't anyone see Mr. Stewart carrying her outside and singing to her? How did he get away with doing this for a whole year?"

"Marilyn, there's no excuse for what Mr. Stewart has done and he will be dealt with, but I can see how he got away with it. Dody is small. She could easily pass for a five-year-old at a distance. Every classroom has an outside door, and Mr. Stewart's class opens to the playground. No one has brought this to my attention, and if they had I would have ended it immediately and Mr. Stewart would have been disciplined and removed from our staff. Didn't Dody tell you what he was doing and what her school day was like?"

Uh oh, now it was back to being Mom's fault. Now her face turns beet red and she yelled, "I have five kids to take care of. I can't keep track of every second of everyone's day, and I have a demanding husband who is going to kill me tonight when he finds out about this. Does he have to find out?" My mom cried uncontrollably and Mrs. Flynn put her arm around her,

"Marilyn, don't you worry, this is going to be taken care of and your husband won't blame you." With her arm still around my mom, we all walked down to Mr. Stewart's room. I followed behind them and was told to stay in the hall while Mrs. Flynn and my mother went into the classroom. I was told nothing when they came out. I couldn't make out what my parents were saying when they fought that night, only that Mr. Stewart's name kept coming up and that goddamn school.

When I wasn't praying to be saved from Mr. Stewart, I talked to God about my fears of living at home. *"When I walked home I froze if I saw a strange car in front of the house. It might be one of Dad's friends. I didn't want to go in the house and I never knew when Mom was going to lock me in the area above the garage. It was hot and dark and had no window. If I screwed the light bulb in it only made it hotter. God, I don't even have a floor to sit on, just long narrow boards with dark space between them. You've seen it. If it's hot outside I know it will be hard to breathe in there and if it's a cool day then I know I'll be okay. Why does my mom hate me? Is this what moms do when they hate their kids? Why do I make her life so hard? She yells at me a lot and she breaks my toys. She makes up stories about me and tells Dad I was bad. I hate his belt. It hurts a lot. I don't know what to do God."*

I didn't always want to be dead. I didn't want to die when school was a good place and I had friends. Everything I loved about it was taken away that year. I lost my friends and I lost my safe place. I couldn't bear to go to school or to go home. I hated being in the storage area above the garage. The entrance to this space was in my bedroom and the door was half the size of a regular one. When Mom told me to go to my room I knew what she meant. I sat on my bed until she came up and opened the dwarf door. I bent over to walk through the door and she locked it behind me always saying, "This is your punishment for being bad."

At first it was scary. I never dropped my feet below the rafter I was sitting on because it looked like a hole with no end. I was afraid of falling and being lost between the boards. After a while I pretended this was my playroom and I started thinking up ways to make it better. One day I found a piece of wood in the garage and snuck it inside. It was much better the next time Mom put me in there. I could lie down and be comfortable. I thought about my new play room all the time and how to make it even more enjoyable, paper and crayons came to mind. I started smuggling all kinds of things to make my punishment time more pleasant. I brought in a doll pillow and blanket for lying down, a small wooden box for drawing on top of and I kept my pencils, paper and crayons inside of the box. My little room would have been perfect if I knew the light bulb could have been switched for a smaller wattage. It was hot in there in the dark and hotter and harder to breath with the light bulb on. Most of my time was spent in the dark, but it was better because I had a board and drew pictures in little spurts.

"God, you're God," I told him. *"You can do anything. Please take me away from here."* Living on Long Island, with three major airports nearby, we had many planes flying over our house. I would lie on the lawn looking up at the belly of a big fat airplane, *"God, please let something fall from that plane and hit me, a tire or a suitcase . . . anything. Please help me, please kill me."* It seemed like such a simple request.

7

The Doctor Is Ready to See You

MR. STEWART, MY THIRD GRADE TEACHER was fired and my parents were ordered to have me evaluated by a doctor as a result of my year with him, hoping that the evaluation would reveal any abuse I may have suffered at the hands of this teacher. My parents did not believe in therapy but had no say in the matter and were forced to take me. My father believed therapists were quacks. Only the spineless and weak went to see them. Those who were so feeble minded—they didn't even know they were seeing a quack.

One Saturday morning, my mom and I got ready to go to New York City. She always took me with her to Gimble's and Macy's when they had a sale. I never looked forward to sale days because I was too small and would get stuck between the tables heaped with clothes and the sea of large monstrous bodies rummaging through piles of fabric. I couldn't breath and sometimes fainted. It's a miracle I was never trampled. On this Saturday morning I figured we were going shopping in the city. Mom frantically circled the parking lot anxious about missing our train. I loved riding the train. I loved any opportunity to pretend I was escaping.

We arrived in the city and walked until my legs ached. We walked past Macy's and we walked by Gimble's.

"Mom, how come we're not going in?"

"Because we're not shopping today. We're going to see someone."

New York City always scared me. It was too dark, always walking in the shadows of the tall gray buildings. I wanted light and color. We walked through the revolving door of a gray, drab building and into the elevator. Again, I was lost among a forest of legs, like tree trunks, and just when I thought I was about to pass out, the door opened. We walked down the hall slowly as Mom counted out the numbers on each door. We stopped in front of the one she was looking for. The numbers 1609 were etched into the glass window framed by an old large wood door. She opened the door and we left the dark corridor and walked into a brightly colored room filled with toys. I had no idea where we were. Why did this room have so many toys in it? A lady with a nice smile and soft voice said, "Mrs. White?"

"Yes, we're here."

"The doctor will be with you soon."

Doctor? What doctor? I was scared. This must be a doctor for kids and that's why there are so many toys in here.

"Mom, am I going to see the doctor?"

"Yes."

"Do I have to take my clothes off?"

"No, he's not that kind of doctor. He's just going to talk to you."

I never heard of a doctor that just talked to you, especially when there wasn't anything wrong with me, unless it was about my fainting. I knew not to ask Mom any more questions. She was getting that look. A big man with a big face and a big smile opened a door and invited my mom and me into his office. He was the biggest man I'd ever seen and he didn't look like a doctor at all. He dressed like the men on the train. He wore a black suit with a white shirt and black tie. He had an office that didn't look like a doctor's exam room.

DODY JOHNSON

It looked like nighttime. The only light came from a lamp on his desk. One wall was darkened with heavy drapes. Two walls were covered in beautiful wood paneling, and one wall had only books on it from floor to ceiling. He had an enormous wood desk in front of the drapes, and the floor was covered in a deep red print carpet. There was a pair of chairs where my mom and I sat at the doctor's desk facing him. Mom and the doctor talked while I examined the room, not paying attention to what they were talking about. In the corner of his office was a cozy sitting area with a large brown leather sofa, a matching chair, and a table between them. There was a coffee table to complete his little living room.

Mom left the office and I was left alone with this big man who towered over me. I was scared being left alone with him.

"Dody, would you like the curtains opened?"

I didn't answer him, and he opened the curtains. I don't know why I decided not to talk. This was out of character for me, I was usually very obedient, and always answered when spoken to. The doctor asked me lots of questions. I wouldn't open my mouth and I didn't know why I was in this room with this strange man. That's all I remember of our first session together.

The next Saturday, Mom and I repeated the steps of the prior Saturday. This time Mom said good-bye when the doctor opened the door. She said she was going shopping. The big man led me into another room. It had more toys in it than the waiting room. We played house, but I still wouldn't open my mouth. He did all the talking. I liked watching him play. I never saw a big man play like that before. I thought when you got big you didn't play with toys, but not this guy; he was really good at it.

Although, he was much too large for the little chair at the table, that didn't stop him. He sat in it anyway. He looked very funny and I wanted to laugh.

"Dody, won't you please sit down and have tea and dessert with me?"

27

I sat down and in the center of the table was a large bowl full of malted milk balls, my favorite!

"Dody, please help yourself to a malt ball." I started to take one and he reached for one also. I pulled my hand back and he ate one. He said again, "Please have a malt ball," and I reached again, so did he. I pulled back and he ate another. We played this game until I think he had a stomach ache. He ate a lot of malt balls and I ate none.

Next, we went to his office to talk. I mean we went to his office and he talked. I was starting to want to talk, but I didn't. Mom arrived and off we went. I still couldn't figure out why I was spending time with this man and why my mother was letting me. It felt very special that we would take a train into the city, walk forever just so I could play with this big man.

We did the same thing the next Saturday. Mom went shopping and I stayed with the big man. This time we spent the whole time in his office, and I was starting to like him. He was funny and nice. He knew how much I loved his big window, so the first thing he did when I walked into his office was open the curtains. We spent a lot of time looking out the window. He told me about all the things he saw and asked me what I saw. I said, "See that lady walking fast in the gray outfit. She has to hurry or they'll catch up with her. See her looking back, she needs to find a place to hide." I started talking to him about the people walking on the sidewalk many floors below us. There were so many people and each one had a story. I told him what they were thinking and where they were going. He showed me some black-and-white pictures. They looked like someone splattered black ink on white cards. He said even though they don't look like much, some people could see pictures in them, like when you look up into the sky and make pictures out of clouds. He asked me what I saw. Mostly, they looked like butterflies or airplanes.

The big man was still asking me a lot of questions, and I remember thinking, I'm going to tell him about Mom and Dad next week. I was scared to tell, but I couldn't think of anything else to do. This man would help me. I trusted him. He wouldn't let anyone hurt me. I thought about telling him then, but it seemed like a lot of time had gone by and Mom would be back soon. No, I better not get started, it won't be good to leave in the middle of telling him. I would tell him first thing when I come back next week. We'd have the whole time to talk about it and decide what to do, and he would tell me what would happen.

I woke up early the next Saturday morning and I'd thought about it all week. I couldn't wait to tell him about Mom and Dad. I didn't want Dad coming to my bedroom at night. I didn't want the "Special Attention." I didn't want to be "Special" alone in the dark with him. I hated most of all watching Artie bleed from his beatings at the bottom of the stairs every Saturday night, and I wanted Mom to stop locking me in the storage area over the garage. I didn't want to be scared anymore, and I believed he would help me. I was also sad—would I be taken from my home? I would miss Artie a lot. But, maybe everyone would be able to leave. Maybe all us kids would live together, and maybe Mom and Dad would go to jail. This also made me sad. The thought of them living behind bars made me think of the animals at the zoo. They looked so trapped and lonely. At times it was too much for me to think about—what would happen to my family if I told? But, the big man kept telling me I could tell him anything and he wouldn't let anybody hurt me even if I told him the biggest secret in the whole wide world. I had to believe he would help my family too. So by the end of the week, I decided I would tell him, and we would just keep it our secret if it meant my family was going to be hurt. In fact, I'd ask him that first.

Seeing the doctor was my window to tell someone what was happening in our home. I had so much I wanted to tell him about my parents and my teacher Mr. Stewart, but I knew there wasn't time to tell it all, so I chose my parents. If I could fix my family or my school, which one would I choose? I chose my family.

Saturday morning found me taking a bath and then putting on my favorite pink dress. It was a party dress that I wore only on special occasions. This was the most special day of my life so I was going to be my prettiest. I put on my white tights and my dress shoes. I wanted to look very pretty in case they took me to a new home. I wanted my new family to like me and see how pretty I was.

After I was all ready, my heart pounding the whole time, I went into the kitchen and Mom was standing next to the counter in her bathrobe.

"Mom, aren't you going to get ready to go to the city?"

"We're not going to the city today."

"Are we going next Saturday?"

"No, we're not going to the doctor's anymore."

I remember the tears rolling down my face as I walked up the stairs to my bedroom. My window to tell had disappeared and so did I for the next three years.

8

Rude Awakening

WHY IS SHE YELLING AT ME? Why am I standing in front of all these kids? I'm frozen. I'm terrified. Who are these kids? They're all so much older than me. Who is this woman and why is she mad at me? I don't recognize this room. I'm dizzy, I feel like I'm going to faint. And, if I don't faint then I'm going to throw up. I hope I faint before I throw up.

I didn't know I was in the sixth grade, or that I was the same age as the kids in the classroom. I didn't know that was my classroom and she was my teacher. I didn't know that I was just waking up after blocking out three years from my life. The month was June and in a few weeks I would graduate from the sixth grade.

"Dody, I know you know your Roman numerals. Write them on the board. Why are you being so difficult? Don't play your hoodlum games with me."

I didn't care how many times she told me I knew them, knowing my Roman numerals seemed the least of my problems. I was paralyzed and I couldn't talk or move.

"Dody, you're not going to get away with this. You want to play games. I'll play games with you. Out, right now. Go to the office. I'll be down after class." I couldn't move. I was still paralyzed, and then she screamed, "Get out, NOW!"

I was startled by the sound of her voice, and I woke up a little more. I slowly walked out of the classroom and into the hall. I didn't know where to go, so I just start walking. I was sick to my stomach. I wasn't just lost in this school; I was lost in my head and nothing made sense. *I was told to go somewhere and I don't know how to get there. Why is that? Why don't I know where I am? Think real hard, how did I get here? How do I leave here? I just want to wake up from this nightmare.* I started walking again. *Maybe I'll find the office.*

A woman approached me in the hall, "May I see your hall pass? You can't be walking around the halls without a pass. What classroom are you in?"

"My teacher told me to go to the office."

"Okay, let's go to the office. Are you sick? Why are you crying?"

We walked into the office and she interrupted the woman running the mimeograph machine behind the counter and told her, "I found this child in the hall. I don't think she feels well."

The hall pass woman left and the office woman started asking me a lot of questions that I didn't know the answers to.

"Honey, what's your teacher's name? What classroom are you in? Are you ill? I think I should call your mother. What's your phone number?" *Where am I? Why don't I know my teacher's name, or what grade I'm in? Why don't I know my phone number?* My eyes were glued to the large picture window behind her. I didn't recognize the scenery.

Next, she asked me a question I knew the answer to, "What's your name?"

"Dody White." She took out my file and found my phone number. She called my home and my mother answered. The office lady said, "Dody is sitting in the office and does not feel well. She looks very pale. How soon can you pick her up?" She turned to me, "Your mother can't leave the house right now, and she would like you to walk home."

I panicked and started crying when I heard my mother wasn't going to pick me up. I heard the woman say in a stern voice, "Mrs. White, you may only live two blocks away, but your daughter is sick and unable to walk home. You need to pick her up now."

My angry mother came to the school and stuck her head in the door and I followed her to the car. The car was different. My mother was different, she use to have brown hair and now it was yellow. She started yelling at me once we left the curb, and I didn't care. She was the first familiar person in this nightmare and that felt better. We drove on streets I never saw before. We drove to a house I never saw before. Inside was furniture I never saw before.

I don't remember what happened after I walked through the front door or how I found my bedroom that first time. My family moved to another city the summer after fourth grade. They purchased a new six-bedroom house and all the furniture in it. That day when I woke up from being gone for three years was the beginning of a pattern I would repeat over and over for the next thirty-three years. I would lose an hour, a week, or months at a time, which kept me in a constant state of confusion. My head ached and I had trouble comprehending. When I woke up at the end of sixth grade, I had repressed the bad memories from age four through eight, my father and his friends touching me, my mother locking me in the storage area. Mr. Stewart's abuse were gone.

I knew I wasn't like most people and that was my secret. I spent most of my life feeling that I was living on the edge of sanity. If people knew that I had such a hard time functioning then I would be evaluated and sent to an institution. I wasn't strong like most people. I kept as quiet as I could without appearing to be weak. I learned that most people liked quiet people. Most people liked to talk and have an audience. I was a good audience. Everybody said I was a good listener. If a person plays it just right, people think you know a lot because you're quiet. They think you're very confident because you never have to prove your point. They think you live by your convictions. If you do it just right, you never have to say a word.

If you're pretty, then people think you're sane. I worked very hard at being pretty. Most people thought I came by it naturally, but not so. The fact that I didn't sleep much gave me lots of time to prepare myself for the world. I ironed my outfit for the day, styled my hair and applied my makeup. With the extra time, I read *Seventeen* magazine and studied how the models made themselves beautiful. I managed to keep myself out of the institutions. I believed two things accomplished that, by not talking and looking pretty.

I lived my life believing this little fantasy. I didn't know that in reality I was quite smart. And that I was a friendly person and easy to be around, that I had a wonderful sense of humor and many creative talents. I didn't know any of this. I thought people liked me because I was quiet and pretty.

9

Big House on the Prairie

THE SUMMER I TURNED ELEVEN, my parents bought a new house built on an old potato field on Long Island. The land was void of green lawns and trees and all the yards were filled with rocks.

Into our third summer at our new home, my older brother, Artie, and I were still raking rocks in our yard. We watched our neighbors lawns slowly turn green and some who were fortunate, had their lawns brought in on a flat bed truck.

One Saturday morning after breakfast, Artie and I went out to rake rocks. The warm summer breeze was delicious as I tasted the salty air from the ocean's potpourri. With our rakes in hand and ready to rid our yard of those pesky little boulders, we heard the roar of something large coming our way. A flatbed truck stopped in front of our neighbor's house, and Mr. Jensen walked out with coffee cup in hand to greet the men in the truck. After a few minutes he went back inside, and before lunch his yard was a lush thick sea of green.

Dad, Artie, and I each had a different reaction to this phenomenon. "I think it's Mr. Jensen's birthday and he's giving himself the ultimate present, a beautiful new yard. It's an excellent gift."

Artie was sad, looking at the Jensen's new lawn.

"I can't believe it. We've been working so hard every summer with no end in sight and abracadabra, the Jensen's have a lawn in four hours. Dad, I've been told the rocks are an acre deep and we'll never get to the end. Can't we have a truck drop off our yard, or at least half of it?"

"Would you like to pay for it? First, a truck load of rich black dirt has to be leveled across the yard and then the sod is rolled out. The dirt, sod, and labor for an installed lawn is very expensive. Other families in the neighborhood are doing it themselves. So can we."

"But, they don't live on a corner. Our yard is twice the size of everyone else's."

Dad was angry. Somehow the Jensens had just shown us up and made us look bad. Their manicured green lawn came right up next to our dirty, rocky one. He seemed to think ours looked better when the Jensen's looked just like it.

"You two are fooling around too much, I want to spread grass seed this summer and see green. I'm tired of looking at dirt and rocks." Dad then went inside to get ready to play a round of golf with Mom.

Under his breath Artie spewed off, "We can't afford it my foot! He can afford the country club and his sports car. Come on, who has a sports car that seats two when you have five kids? He can afford Broadway plays and dinners in expensive restaurants. I don't get it. You'd think he would want the lawn to look good, at least for appearances."

Raking rocks was our summer entertainment. I think that's why I enjoyed reading books about the pioneers. I was attracted to the life style where husband and wife worked side by side in the fields together. I loved how they shared the same passion for their home and land. In my world, I was pretending that I was on the prairie preparing the soil for seed.

So, Artie and I raked the rocks. He hated it, but I loved the time with him. He was always clowning around and making me laugh. He loved to entertain me and I was his biggest fan. We often thought we were done clearing an area by putting all the rocks into a pile, only to find more rocks where we had just raked. I think he was right, the rocks were an acre deep.

After we raked the rocks into piles, we loaded them into the wheelbarrow and Artie pushed it two long blocks to a vacant lot. I felt sorry for the people who would build their house on the lot where everyone dumped their rocks. We talked and laughed and passed fathers with their wheelbarrows on the way to and from the vacant lot. We were the only kids pushing a wheelbarrow, and we received lots of praise from the other dads for doing such a good job. I loved that part. Sometimes Artie would let me ride in the wheelbarrow on the way back. He said I was lighter than the rocks.

Near the end of three summers raking rocks, we completed the job and the land was ready for seed. Dad walked around the yard with the spreader, and my job was to move the sprinkler to saturate the ground with water. Everyday I looked for grass to break through and then one day while I was riding my bike, I saw our yard at a distance. It had a faint haze of light green across it. Soon the grass grew thick and dark. It was gorgeous. Although Dad never said anything, I knew our yard was beautiful because of Artie and me, and I felt proud. In my prairie fantasy, I was satisfied that we had a good crop that year.

10

Decorating Prodigy

FOR A MONTH I WORKED ON MY PROJECT to move all us kids into different bedrooms. My dad taught me how to draw three dimensional and interior floor plans when I was six. I loved drawing the double lines and deciding where to put the doors and windows. It was Saturday night and my parents had plans for the evening. They still went to the weekly neighborhood party in Garden City, only they didn't live in the neighborhood anymore and had to drive to it. I knew they wouldn't be home before dawn. Kathy, sixteen, and Artie, fourteen, were spending the night at a friend's house, and I, now eleven years old, was left to watch Billy and Bobby. This was the perfect night to take my plans from paper and create what I had designed. I was anxious to get started.

Dad went to school to be an architect and we shared the same passion for building and interior design. He always said, "When you graduate from high school, you'll want to go to interior design school to be a decorator. You won't learn much and hopefully the school won't take away your natural talent, but the credentials will open doors for you to work in the design field." Dad supported me one-hundred percent when it came to decorating so there was no doubt in my mind that he wouldn't love this project and shower me with lots of praise.

I looked at the clock in the kitchen, it was five. I had about eleven hours to complete this job with probably time to spare. "Billy and Bobby, I'm going to move all us kids into a different bedroom. How does that sound to you?"

"Great! Can we still share a room together?"

"Yes, of course."

"Which room is going to be ours?"

"I'm going to move you to this room across the hall from the bathroom and Kathy is going to have the room next door."

"That's your room. Where's your new room?"

"At the end of the hall next to Kathy's room."

"Where will Artie's new room be if you're in his room?"

"I'm going to put him in Kathy's old room downstairs."

"Why? He'll be the only one downstairs. Will he like that?"

"He'll love it. Artie has the most stuff so he needs the largest room. Downstairs he'll be able to play his music longer in the evening without bothering anyone." Looking back, I think I placed Artie in that room so he would be the farthest from Dad and maybe Dad would forget about him and stop hurting him so much.

When I started moving the furniture, Billy asked, "How come you're not moving Mom and Dad into a different room?"

"Because they have a special room in the house just for them. They're the parents, so they have the room with the big walk-in closet and private bathroom."

"Oh, yeah, that makes sense."

I worked on Billy and Bobby's new room first. All three of us started clearing out the spare room and putting the contents in the living room. I ran their bath water and they grabbed their pajamas. While they took their bath I moved them from the room next door into their new room. By the time they finished their bath all the furniture was moved into its new location and I was sweeping the floor, putting clean sheets on the beds, standing on their dressers to hang their curtains and polishing their furniture. Billy and Bobby sat at the top of the stairs with their evening snack watching me work.

It wasn't easy moving all that furniture up and down the stairs. Dressers were the hardest, mattresses the easiest. Kathy had the biggest furniture, and in order to move her long nine-drawer dresser, I had to take the drawers out and put a blanket under all the legs and slide it to the bottom of the stairs. I pushed it up the carpeted treads upside down, laid the blanket on the landing and pivoted the dresser to the bottom of the six stairs left to conquer. Again, I pushed it up the stairs on its top until I reached the upper floor level. I slid her dresser down the hall still upside down on the blanket into her new bedroom.

I repeated this over and over until I placed all of the furniture in its new location. The most painful part was getting shocked all the time from constantly rubbing against the carpet. Billy and Bobby got a kick out of watching me make sparks and burst out laughing every time I lit up.

I hated moving the furniture, but I had to do it to get to the decorating part. Kathy's room was the most challenging because she had the fewest things to work with. I wanted to change her room from looking like the stark exam room at the medical clinic into a friendly and comfortable place for her and her friends.

I discovered she kept all her favorite things in her closet. She had books, a stuffed animal that a boy won for her at the fair, a jewelry box and little glass figurines. They were so delicate, from half an inch to an inch tall. She had ten little boxes filled with miniature animals. I had no idea she collected these little creatures. Why did she keep her favorite things hidden? I brought everything out to be seen. I wanted her room to look like an expression of who she was, and not like a place where sick people went. She didn't have a bedspread so I gave her one of mine.

Artie's room was the exact opposite. He had too much stuff, and his room was jam-packed. Artie had many interests—music, reading, writing and numerous collections. He played the trumpet and guitar, and had stacks of sheet music. He had notebooks full of music he'd written himself. He collected everything from comic books to musical instruments. He had drums, tambourines, and maracas. Artie's room improved the most because I replaced his piles of stuff with designated areas—a place for his musical instruments with a place to play them, a comfortable reading area plus a writing area. I made sure his desk was cleared and organized so his mind was free from clutter and open to write songs.

In the wee hours of the morning, my parents drove into the driveway and stared at the house bewildered. There was something peculiar and they couldn't figure out what it was. They talked about whether or not they were at the right house. It didn't help that they had just spent the evening drinking, and they were sleep deprived, or that every other house looked the same. It took a while, but Mom finally figured it out. "Art, look at the curtains. They look like our curtains, but they're on different windows." They came inside once they decided they were home. Billy, Bobby and I were sound asleep.

When my parents woke up after a few hours sleep, they walked around the house and looked at all the new bedrooms. They were in a good mood and laughing about sitting in the car that morning trying to figure out if they were home or not. They liked all the new bedrooms and thought I did a great job.

"Dad, can I do the rest of the house?"

"Show me your plans first and don't even think about moving our bedroom."

I asked Artie and Kathy many years later why they weren't angry with me for changing their bedrooms around. They were teenagers, and moving their rooms meant I had to touch all their

41

stuff. Kathy said, "I liked the change, and my new room always looked better than the old one."

"Why did you keep all your favorite things hidden in your closet?"

"Because I didn't want Mom to find them and throw them out when she got mad at me."

"Why didn't you hide them again, after I brought them out?"

"I liked my new room. It was more comfortable and a nicer place to be in when my friends came over, so I decided to take a chance."

Artie added, "Not only did I get a new room, I also got a clean one."

I was glad they were okay with what I did, but now looking back, I think as a family we were beyond dysfunctional with absolutely no boundaries at all. No one felt ownership of their things or their space to care if someone came in and changed it all around without asking first.

11

Rearranging the Neighborhood

I STARTED BABYSITTING AT THE AGE OF ELEVEN. I used my babysitting money to buy things to decorate my bedroom, like paint, wallpaper, or a picture. Sometimes I bought a new bedspread with matching curtains and I always loved fresh flowers in my room.

For fifty cents an hour, not only did I baby-sit but I also cleaned and cooked. I cleaned because I couldn't stand a messy house. The cooking, I didn't love so much.

Every Wednesday and Saturday evening I had a standing babysitting job at the Spears's home across the street from us. The Spears were not well liked in the neighborhood. As much as their neighbors tried, Mr. and Mrs. Spears would not engage in conversation when caught outside for a few moments. The rumor was that Mr. Spear was in the mafia. Now why would a family who wanted to keep to themselves, move into a busy, active neighborhood like ours? The Spears had four children: Marvin and Rachel, who were elementary school age, and two newborn twins Stephen and Thomas.

On a typical evening, I arrived at their home, made dinner, cleaned up the kitchen and prepared the kids for bed. With everyone asleep, I sat in the family room uncomfortable in my surroundings. The Spears still had packed boxes in all the rooms and pictures leaning against walls. The furniture was scattered throughout the house in the same place the moving men dropped it. I couldn't stand looking at their home unattended to any longer. They'd lived here for two years and that's too long to still look like you've just moved in. No one was in charge of getting the house in order, so I decided to take it on. My head hurt if a room was too messy or disorganized, and at the Spears house, I always had a headache. I believe that's why I needed to decorate. Inside, I felt pain and confusion. By making a room beautiful and pleasing to my eyes, my mind rested and I felt better.

One Saturday late in the afternoon I went over to the Spears to baby-sit. After dinner, with the kitchen cleaned up and the twins sound asleep, I asked Marvin and Rachel, "Would you like to have new beautiful bedrooms?" They both said, "Yes" and jumped up and down with excitement. The Spears lived in the Americana, same floor plan as ours, so I knew it well.

I moved the kids into different bedrooms, just like I had done in my house. We arranged the furniture and polished it. I hung Rachel's ballet shoes on the wall next to her picture of the ballerina. Now, instead of taking up space on the floor accumulating dust, they had meaning and importance on the wall. It was a nice touch.

We unpacked Marvin's model airplane collection and arranged them on a bookcase I gave him from the living room. His eye's lit up when he saw his planes displayed. He was so proud of his collection. Marvin was also very nervous. "I don't think Mom will like taking the bookcase out of the living room. I think we better put it back."

"I think your mom will like it a lot. They weren't even using it in the living room. And if she doesn't like it I'll put it back."

I found curtains and rods and hung them after I found the tools. Finally, I vacuumed the whole house. The kids were walking zombies by now. Decorating was hard work. They loved their new bedrooms and couldn't wait to sleep in them, which they did as soon as their heads hit their pillows.

I looked in on the twins when I heard them fussing. After I changed their diapers and gave them warm formula, they were sound asleep again.

Next, I worked on the family room, living room, and dining room. I moved furniture from the upstairs living room to the downstairs family room. I reorganized the kitchen cupboards. Plastic containers, glasses, and food had been thrown into the shelves, and sat wherever they landed, just like the way their furniture was placed in the house. *I can't wait until they see their new home. They're going to love it. And if they don't love it, what's the worse that can happen? I'll have to put everything back the way it was. But I think they're going to love it. At least everything is out of the boxes now.* After all the furniture was arranged, I hung the pictures. At 3:30 in the morning I polished the furniture just before conking out. I was sound asleep when Mrs. Spears woke me up at 5:30. She paid me, and barely awake, I walked across the street to my bed.

That afternoon the phone rang and Mom yelled, "Dody, Mrs. Spears wants to see you right away."

Oh, my God, what did I do? Why did I do it? How could I have been so bold to rearrange their house? I moved Marvin and Rachel into different rooms. I hung pictures on their walls. I decorated their home without their permission. What was I thinking? What possessed me to do that? I pictured myself walking into the Spears home with the police waiting for me. *If Mr. Spears is part of the Mafia, I don't think he would call the police. I hope he's with the Mafia.*

I rang the doorbell and Mrs. Spears yelled, "Come in, Dody. I'm feeding the twins." I walked into the house. No police. When I entered the kitchen, Mrs. Spears had the friendliest grin on her face.

"The house is beautiful. How did you know how to do it? I love this picture here and this table next to the couch, and I never would have thought to use this old beat up family trunk as a coffee table. It looks great. Every room is beautiful and the kitchen is organized. I have just one question, why didn't you do the twins room?"

"Because they are infants and there are two of them. I thought it was very important for you to know where everything is, so I didn't touch anything in there."

"Can we do their room now?" We started moving cribs and changing tables and dressers, with Mrs. Spears letting me make all the decisions.

Mrs. Spears, who never talked to anyone before started telling her neighbors what her babysitter did. Word got around the neighborhood that I was talented in decorating and I watched from my bedroom window as people paraded through the Spears front door to see what the eleven-year-old babysitter did.

A couple weeks later the Spears had an underground sprinkler system installed. The landscapers came and planted shrubs and trees and lined the stone path to the front door with green plants and colorful flowers. Last, they laid the sod. I like to think I inspired them.

Mothers in the neighborhood started calling me to look at their homes for help with furniture arranging, picture hanging and picking out colors. Not bad for an eleven-year-old. I found my talent and I knew I wanted to be an interior decorator when I grew up. The Spears house was the first time I decorated outside my home.

12

Cattaraugus, New York

O NE MONTH BEFORE MY FOURTEENTH BIRTHDAY, my family moved from Long Island to Cattaraugus, a small town in western New York, fifty miles south of Buffalo. My father quit his job as a district salesman for Johns-Manville in Manhattan, and accepted the sales manager position at U.S. Plywood in Cattaraugus. He loved his job at J-M and was one of a few being considered for the sales manager position that opened up.

When Dad worked at J-M he spent months preparing for a business trip to meet with a new prospective customer. This would be a large account to land and if he closed the deal, it would give him the recognition he had long been waiting for. At the last minute, the day before Dad was to leave, his boss, Mr. Kotter, decided he better go instead. This account was too important to send a salesman. Mr. Kotter never made it to the meeting. The plane crashed and all passengers on board were killed.

For the next year, Dad and I visited the Kotter's home in Connecticut many times, helping Mrs. Kotter with the endless paperwork and all the details that needed attending to. During that year, Dad did his work plus his deceased boss's work and didn't doubt he would receive the promotion. The day he found out they offered it to someone else, he quit.

Dad loved a good challenge, and after he settled down from the initial shock of not getting the promotion and finding himself without a paying job, he started hunting for a new employer. He subscribed to all the major cities newspapers from coast to coast. His plan was to send out 500 resumes every week. He went through all the classifieds and put a check mark next to the positions he was interested in. Once he finished going through all the papers he started typing his cover letter to each company. I helped him stuff envelopes with cover letter and his resume. Next, we applied the postage and off to the post office we went. By the time we mailed out his quota for the week, the new papers started arriving at the house. I was Dad's right-hand person and he explained to me in great depth how to find the right job. Mom told me years later Dad had a Plan B. If he didn't land a job in six months, he was going to take his life and have it look like an accident so we would be taken care of from his life insurance.

My father had a good resume showing his accomplishments with well-known corporations and it didn't take long for him to land work again. He went to first and second interviews across the country, and told us all about the places he visited when he came home. We talked about learning to surf when he went to California and skiing if we moved to Colorado. I was hoping for a place near the ocean. I have fond memories during the time my father was unemployed. Looking for a job was more than a full-time job, it took seven days a week of Dad's time. This unplanned interruption changed our family for a while. We talked excitedly about new places we might move to and I wonder if we were all thinking, the unknown was much more appealing than the way our life had been. We knew Dad was getting close to securing a job when U.S. Plywood called him back for his third interview. I loved hearing the stories about Cattaraugus. We never lived in a small town before and it sounded like moving to another country. Dad told us Cattaraugus was a village surrounded by large beautiful hills, dairy farms and an Amish community. He described how on Main Street, we'd see laundry strung across front porches, and I had visions of Appalachia.

I will never forget the summer afternoon we drove into Cattaraugus. Dad was right, I saw laundry hanging on front porches. But there was nothing poor looking about this village. It sat in a valley surrounded by large rolling hills. The streets were red brick and lined with huge maple trees. The houses were large and stately, historical and gorgeous. Almost every house had a fresh coat of white paint. The grand church, decked out in red brick, sat in the center of town ringing her bells so loud you could hear them everywhere. They rang on the hour and half hour so we always knew what time it was. I felt like I had just entered paradise. Cattaraugus, in her simplistic grandeur, was a breath of fresh air. I think I would have disappeared forever if we had stayed on Long Island where my confusion was increasing, I felt lost most of the time and I still didn't want to be on this planet.

Christine Boone knocked at our front door our second day in Cattaraugus. She was my age and her father was the assistant principal at the high school. She welcomed me to town and we walked for blocks as she told me about this quaint little place.

Although Cattaraugus was relatively small with a population of 1,200, a division of U.S. Plywood was located there and that consisted of four manufacturing plants plus the main office. People came from Buffalo and Jamestown to work at U.S. Plywood.

This small village had many churches and three private clubs with swimming pools named Wildwood, Skyline, and Rycola. At first I thought it strange that a village this size had three mini country clubs, but I soon learned it was part of what made this community shine and work well together. Everything about Cattaraugus was tidy, decent and in order. Everyone knew who they were and they were comfortable in their place. No one went without and everyone helped each other. Cattaraugus had heart and I felt it.

Our family was invited to join Rycola, the white-collar club. It was a gathering place, and many parties and celebrations were held there throughout the year. During the summer, moms spent the day at the pool with their kids and the dads joined them after work for cocktails and to grill the family dinner over hot coals.

The middleclass club was Skyline. They had the best view sitting on top of a hill overlooking the village. Wildwood was the blue-collar club where all the town picnics and class reunions were held because they had the largest land that accommodated volleyball and horse shoe throwing.

All the clubs were equipped with his and her bathrooms, showers, fully furnished kitchens and large stone fireplaces. I loved Rycola, and it provided a great place for slumber parties year round.

My parents bought a stately Tudor-style house with three fireplaces, lots of beveled-glass windows, custom woodwork through out with dark rich paneling traveling three quarters up the wall towards the high ceilings with crown moldings. There was a wine cellar in the basement, a wrap around staircase with a large beveled-glass window at the midway landing and a tennis court in the side yard. I took tennis lessons, and Artie and I played after dinner with friends joining us often.

On the first day of school I walked down to the art room and told Mrs. Olson the art teacher, I wanted to be an interior designer. She said, "All right, the school you want to go to is the Art Institute of Pittsburgh. They have the best design program in the country, and it's their school all the major firms look to for their new hires. I'll work with you over the next four years so you'll have everything you need for your portfolio to take with you to your interview."

I never tired of walking around town. At night when it was dark, I loved watching the bats above me fly from treetop to treetop. Every so often Artie and I walked to the edge of town where the garbage dump was located. We looked down from the hillside and gazed at the bears going through their treasures below us. In the spring, I loved seeing the huge maple trees lining both sides of main street holding buckets to capture the sap to make maple syrup. In the winter I enjoyed riding on the back of a snowmobile high on a hill in a farmer's pasture overlooking Cattaraugus nestled in her valley. It always took my breath away. Cattaraugus had a slow life style that set well with my spinning head and offered me an opportunity to connect with people.

I received instant popularity in Cattaraugus. How the girls talked me into trying out for cheerleading and how I made it was a miracle! I was not an athletic person. I could do a summersault, ride a bike, swim, play tennis and not much more. Now that I was a cheerleader, I learned to do cartwheels and splits, and I discovered endorphins. It wasn't long before I was addicted to exercise. We lived a block from the high school, so every morning at five o'clock I ran around the football field eight times. I started every day on a high from running, and it helped get me through the day. When I had time alone, I spent that time writing about how wonderful death would be.

I was most confused during my school day, my head was in a fog and often the halls spun as I went from class to class. I could not comprehend my teacher's lessons. I took algebra twice and worked with my teacher after school trying to understand X, Y and pi. I was fascinated with biology but couldn't grasp the isms and the labels on everything. My favorite class was English because I loved to write, but why was it I couldn't remember how to use verbs and adjectives? It was in my junior year English class that I realized what was causing some of my learning disability.

One day Mrs. Berry was walking around the classroom talking about the different parts to a sentence and I found it utterly interesting. She walked to the blackboard and turned to write a sentence and I blacked out. When I came to she was sitting at her desk and the chalkboard was full of writing. I remember it was a clean slate before I passed out and now it was covered with words. The next day in class Mrs. Berry walked around the room and again I was engaged with her lecture. I loved listening to her soft voice and her choice of words. As she told her story she turned to face the chalkboard and I panicked inside. *No! Not now. Don't write on the chalkboard. I want to hear the story,* and then I disappeared. At this point I thought I just had a problem with chalkboards. I couldn't figure out why and I didn't dare tell anyone. If I did, it would only get me closer to the institution. I would rather be sick and out in the world then live in a room behind bars.

Throughout my high school years I kept popping up in places and I didn't know how I got there. One day I appeared on the side lawn at the high school in my cheerleader uniform and we were practicing routines. I sat down on the grass and pretended I was listening to Christine explain our next routine as I tried to remember the last couple hours. The last thing I remembered was sitting in science wearing my peach-colored slacks and light-brown sweater. What happened between the time I was sitting in science class to being here? When did I change into my uniform? I showed up at places and didn't remember how I got there. I didn't like to think about losing time for an hour or two and I tried my best to not disappear, but I could not control it.

I was lucky that my life in high school kept me busy. I had cheerleading practice and all the games to go to. I was in most of the school plays and chorus recitals and that involved a lot of practice time. I went to proms, winter balls, and school dances.

Everyone was popular in Cattaraugus. A school needed more than just the cheerleaders; we needed the athletes and the fans to watch the game and students to work the concession stand. That was Cattaraugus, everyone contributed to make sports happen.

The "everyone involved concept" also applied to plays and recitals with actors and singers needed. Students made costumes, created stages and sold tickets and advertising for the printed program. The last position filled was the audience made up of the town's people. Everyone had something to do. I was too busy with outside activities to decorate my parent's house like I'd been doing before we moved from Long Island. But, once a year, I designed a new bedroom for myself and when my parents hosted a party, Dad brought guests upstairs to show off my new creation.

Although my life was filled with activities including the weekly date and slumber parties with the girls, staying alive was becoming more unbearable. I don't know what would have happened to me if my family hadn't moved to this paradise in the valley.

13

Violence in a Public Place

CATTARAUGUS WAS NOT A SAVING PLACE for my parents. Life in our new village brought on a new level of violence for them. Weekdays were bad, weekends were worse, and on holidays all hell broke loose. Weekdays you beat your wife, weekends you beat your kids, and on holidays everyone was fair game. During the holidays was when most things got broken, like dishes, furniture, and bones, and Mom still loved throwing the dinner plates on the ceiling. She wasn't funny anymore and seemed to have left her sense of humor on Long Island. Dad was busy with his career, golf, and becoming part of the Cattaraugus community. I think Mom felt lost and left out. She spent a lot of time in bed.

A few weeks before my sixteenth birthday, Dad planned a two-week-long business trip to California for six men, their wives, and children. The first week was all business for the men during the day, and their wives joined them in the evening for dinner and socializing. The second week was all vacation time and everyone was free to spend the time however they planned to use it.

On the last day of the business part of the trip, after five nights of eating out and drinking into the wee hours of the morning, Mom said, "Art, I'm exhausted. I'm going to skip the socializing tonight and have dinner in the room with the kids. I just want to take a hot bath and relax."

"Why don't you do that and take a short nap. I'll call you when we're ready to sit down for dinner and you can join us."

"Not tonight. I don't have it in me."

Dad replied before closing the door behind him, "I'll see you in a few hours." It must be time for dinner because our phone kept ringing. Mom gave us strict orders not to answer it. Next, Dad was pounding on our door. "Marilyn, open the door." She opened the door, and he smacked her on the back of her head. "Get ready, quick. Dinner is being served." She changed out of her pajamas and into an evening dress and accompanied Dad to dinner. Hours later Mom came running into the room and put the chain across the door. "No matter what happens, do not open this door." Soon after she said that, my father came to the door and started banging on it, "Unlock the door, Marilyn, I'm going to kill you." *That will give her incentive to open the door.* Dad had the door open as far as the chain would allow and he was holding a large meat cleaver. I wrapped my arms around Billy and Bobby, trying to protect them as we hunkered down in the corner farthest from the door and out of Dad's sight. I prayed fast and hard, *Mom, don't open the door.* I knew if she did, he would kill her and maybe us also. I blacked out hearing my mother and father screaming at each other and the knife hitting the door repeatedly.

When I woke up the next morning, my mother was alive. Dad wasn't in the room and the door was still locked. Mom wasn't with us for the rest of the trip. Her body was present, but she wasn't. We walked around Disneyland that day and I wondered why my mother was in her withdrawn state. I'd lost the memory of what transpired the night before. It would be thirty years before I remembered that evening.

During the second week we traveled through California from Disneyland to San Francisco with many stops along the way. One evening while walking down Fisherman's Wharf, I, looked forward to seeing Alcatraz across the water. Dad poked his head into a bar and said, "It's time. Let's go in and watch." We walked into the darkened bar and looked up at the TV to see Neil Armstrong walking on the moon. He positioned the flag and recited his famous words, "That's one small step for a man, one giant leap for mankind."

Mom rarely went to social events after that California trip, and she and Dad ceased doing things together. I became Dad's golf partner and his escort when he went to nightclubs. He was an enthusiastic fan of professional performers. He often invited them to our table during their breaks and many became friends of the family and spent time at our house. Maybe Dad was trying to find a new set of friends after that California trip.

One winter afternoon I was skiing at Holiday Valley, a ski resort near Cattaraugus, when I saw Dad standing on the deck of the chalet watching me. He waved and a chill went through my body. It felt eerie seeing him standing there. I knew at that moment my dad was obsessed with me and we were spending too much time together. I didn't want to be my mother's replacement.

A few years after I graduated from school, I ran into Marcia on the street. "Dody, do you have a few minutes to visit?"

"Yes," and I followed her inside her home. Marcia was one of the wives on the California trip.

"Dody, has anyone ever told you what happened that night in the hotel dining room when your father acted insane?"

"No. What happened?" I didn't remember my father acting insane and found her story intriguing. It did explain to me why my mother and father stopped doing things together and why their social life changed so abruptly.

"We had just finished eating and your mother stood up to leave. She told us she was tired and calling it an early night. Your dad went over and put his arm around her and said, 'Marilyn, it's our last night here. You'll have plenty of time to catch up on your sleep next week.' Your mom started screaming at the top of her lungs, broken sentences with lots of swear words, pounding her fist on the dining room table while jumping up and down. Your dad also lost it and threw vulgarities back at her. He was beyond drunk at that point from pounding down drinks for hours. After hotel management came in to try and quiet both of them, your father started chasing your mother and we lost site of them after she ran into the kitchen with him close behind her. Security took your father away from your door that night and put him in another room with a guard posted outside. He passed out as soon as he hit the bed.

"That evening I witnessed the worst display of tempers I ever saw two people act out. Your dad was incoherently drunk and your mother was crazy. The consensus in the neighborhood after that trip was she drove him to his madness. Whenever there was a party in town, most people didn't want your mother there. She scared too many of us who'd seen her rage acted out on that trip and we didn't want to see it again."

"Thank you for telling me." After some small talk, I left and I thought to myself, *good, someone besides us kids saw how our parents behaved.*

Kathy stayed on Long Island when we moved to Cattaraugus. Artie was a senior the year we moved there and went to college on Long Island the next year. He visited a few times and on his last trip home, after witnessing another weekend of violence, he said to Mom and Dad, "I don't know why I come home. It's never good. I don't have to watch your demented ways anymore. You two make me sick." He hugged Bill, Bob, and me good-bye and drove away.

As I got older, I started to understand my parents' fighting. I heard their insecurities as they yelled stupid things. Clearly, they didn't like each other or their sad, unfulfilling lives. Dad worked hard, and all he wanted at the end of the day was to sit in his chair, have a scotch and be left alone. Bill, Bob, and I left him alone just fine, but Mom wouldn't. No matter how many times he said, "Not now, Marilyn," she continued. Why should he be able to relax when she couldn't? So they drank together until their attacks went from words to fists. After Mom was quieted by a hard hit, she retreated to their bedroom, and Dad poured another scotch and passed out in his chair.

I hated holidays. It didn't matter if it was Halloween or Christmas, they all ended in tears, screaming and things broken again; dishes, furniture, toys and our spirits. The world outside our home was preparing us for a special festivity, and we always bought into it. We thought it was going to visit our house just like everyone else's.

The world expected my parents to decorate the house and buy presents and we had to have holiday clothes. In our parent's minds we already had too much. My siblings and I knew not to ask for anything, but the world was making my parents do things they didn't want to do. Their anger again turned to rage and our presents always came with a price.

On most holidays from the time I was young until I left my parents' home, they sent us to our rooms and behind our closed doors we sat afraid and alone, hoping they wouldn't call out our name. When my parents tired of hurting each other, it was time for the children to be punished for being so selfish with our "give me" attitude. How could we be sad after they had just spent all this money on us, and decorated the F------ house and made the F------- Christmas cookies? How did we dare not show our appreciation? My parents created the terrifying situation and then berated us for being scared. By the time the holiday arrived, all we wanted was for it to be over.

Although I stayed present during the holidays growing up and aware of the violence that filled our home, it wasn't until I left that I would disappear during those celebrations. It didn't matter if it was Halloween or Christmas. Every year I was triggered by the music and the festivities, and I disappeared during that time. From the age of eighteen to forty-five I have very little memory of a holiday.

Cattaraugus offered me a lot of saving grace but not enough to overcome my parents' violence.

14

George and Gracie's Last Fight

IT WAS A SUNDAY MORNING EARLY IN OCTOBER, three years after we moved to Cattaraugus, when my dad bestowed on my mom his last act of violence. Kathy and Artie lived on Long Island, and Bill, Bob, and I were left at home with these two lunatics.

I was seventeen, a senior in high school, and my parents were having one of their fights again, only this one wasn't ending. Mom and Dad started fighting the night before, and ten hours later it was still going strong. None of us slept that night, and I stayed with the boys in their room as we listened to yelling, pounding from furniture being thrown and glass smashing against the walls. By morning Bill couldn't stop shaking and said, "Something bad is going to happen. I just know something bad is going to happen. This is the big one."

I think we all knew this might be their last fight and we were terrified of the next few hours. Bob was frozen like an icicle, as if he would break if he moved. Bill just turned twelve and Bob was nine. They looked so small with their blond hair and little angelic faces, now vulnerable and full of fear. I wanted to scream at my parents, "STOP! Can't you stop fighting?" I hugged my brothers and told them it will be over soon, but that wasn't happening.

The sun was coming up and Dad yelled, "Marilyn, where's the rope?" Immediately I pictured my father hanging himself from the rafters in the garage and I hoped with all my heart he would.

At 6:30 I said, "Let's get dressed and go up town for breakfast." With that little statement, both of them let out a gasp of air, as if they had been holding their breath and forgot how to breathe. Bob moved and spoke, "I like that idea." While we were dressing to leave, Dad screamed "Marilyn, where's the F------ rope?" He was completely unaware of how much he needed her.

We walked outside, and the sun filled our faces with warm, welcoming light. We smiled at each other. It was good to be out. We didn't talk about our parents. Instead, we talked about normal people.

"Bob, how's your new coach this year? Do you like him?"

"Yeah, he's good. I'm hitting better."

"When's your next game?"

"Tuesday at four."

"I look forward to it. Bill, what have you and Kevin been up to?"

"We're working on an engine in the garage."

"Wow, do you know how to work on an engine?"

"No, but it's fun anyway."

For me that fall morning there was no better place in the world to take a walk than in Cattaraugus. I loved the large sidewalks showing off her age and being aware of generations before me walking the same path. The streets lined with half-naked maple and oak trees with their leaves floating through the air vibrant with colors framing the beautiful homes with manicured lawns. We exchanged greetings with Mr. Mitchell as he gathered the Sunday paper off his front porch.

We walked into Luce's Restaurant and took a booth next to a window. I felt safe and the boys were calm. I loved the greetings from everyone, and I especially liked it when someone asked, "What brings you three up here so early?" I thought, *someone actually cares that we're alive. We should come here every morning for breakfast.* I also felt sad. I sat in the booth enjoying the town's people and breathing in the sweet aromas from the kitchen while my father was probably hanging himself over Bill's engine in the garage.

Dad found the rope while we were gone. Mom was dazed from his punches, and he tightly wrapped a blanket around her. He took the rope and tied her to her favorite chair in the living room. Next, he used his Zippo to light the blanket and left her alone to die.

Mom started screaming as flames surrounded her. Our next door neighbor heard the screams and ran into the house and extinguished the fire. When the boys and I arrived home, Mrs. Reardon came out the back door and whispered to me, "There has been an incident." It was an incident, all right, but not the one I'd been imagining. I followed Mrs. Reardon into the house. Our home looked like it had been visited by a tornado. I walked over broken furniture, glass, and the curtains lying on the floor. Books were everywhere. Nothing was in its place.

We walked into the living room and I began to cry. On the floor near Mom's favorite chair were the charred rope and the remains of the burned blanket. Mrs. Reardon told me how she found my mother in flames tied to her chair. "Thank God the drapes were on the floor nearby. I was able to use them to smother the fire." Seeing Mom's broken wing-back chair upset me the most. Did Dad break it before he tied her in it? Did it break when she came to and was trying to escape? It looked like a pile of garbage on the floor and just moments ago, my mother was in it.

"Where's Mom?"

"In bed." Slowly I walked up the stairs as thoughts raced in my head. *Is this what it's come down to, who can kill the other one first? Where are you, Dad? What state of mind are you in? I hate you,*

you bastard! You don't need help. There's nothing wrong with you. I'm glad life is going so well for you. Are you coming back? I entertained the thought that he might never come back.

Mom was lying in bed motionless, drained of life. Her face was swollen, turning shades of purple and blue. Her eyes were red, puffy and misted over. Tears were streaming down her cheeks.

"Mom, will you leave him now?"

"I'm seriously thinking about it."

I gently hugged my mother, "I love you."

The next day, Mom, Bill, Bob, and I went to a hotel in Olean, New York, thirty miles from Cattaraugus. We left the house in shambles just the way it was. I was relieved Mom didn't make us clean it up. We stayed at the hotel for two weeks. When we first arrived, Mom asked me to call my boyfriend's grandmother who lived across the street from our house. Jesse, my boyfriend, and I had dated on and off over the past three years and were on at the moment. I loved his grandmother, Meredith English, who always had a funny story to tell or something interesting to show me.

I called. "Mrs. English, my brothers and I are at a hotel in Olean with my mother. She and my father had a big fight yesterday and Dad walked out. Mom thought getting away for a little while would be good for everyone. Will you call her when you see my dad has returned?"

"Yes, I'll be happy to watch the house. Tell your mom I'll call her when Art is back."

"Thank you. Bye."

"Take care."

Mom saw an attorney on the fourth day we were in Olean. When she came back I asked, "How did it go Mom?"

"I have a lot to think about."

"What did the attorney say?"

"He said I was lucky this time. Next time I might not be so lucky. He said there's only one smart thing to do and that's divorce."

"Great, are you going to?"

"Like I said, I have a lot to think about. I was in that fight too. I was just as bad as your father. This guy just wants to make money off another divorce."

"Mom, Dad tried to kill you."

"He was drunk. We were both drunk. I don't want to talk about it anymore."

Meredith called Mom the second week we were away, "Marilyn, Art is back at the house."

Mom handed the phone to me. I asked, "Mrs. English, may I come and stay with you for a while?"

"Sure, honey, will your mom be all right?"

"She says she will. I'll be there tomorrow afternoon. Thank you. Bye."

Mom wanted me to stay with Mrs. English so I could spy on my father and I did. I arrived the next afternoon, and Mrs. English and I had a long talk about my parent's marriage. I kept my mother's confidence and didn't tell her how bad the fight was or what condition the house was in. I watched Dad leave the house every morning in his business suit, come home for lunch and again at five o'clock. I called Mom everyday with a report. It looked like he was cleaning and fixing up the house. Mrs. English watched with me each evening. We couldn't see what Dad was doing through the shears he hung over the windows, but Mrs. English made me laugh giving a play by play of his shadow moving around from room to room. "What the heck is he doing in there moving around so much? It's like he's dancing throughout the house. I never saw someone move so much in all my life."

It took a year after that incident, but finally they were done. After twenty-five years of threatening to do so, Mom left Dad.

15

Corinth, My New Family

IN THE FALL OF MY SENIOR YEAR my best friend, Karla, and I drove to Pittsburg for my interview at the Art Institute. I brought my big, fat, black portfolio filled with three years of work preparing for this interview. That winter I received word that I was accepted into their Interior Design program.

The next year classes started at the institute. I didn't go. The memory of my father's last act of violence against my mother escaped my conscious mind soon after he tried to kill her. I wondered for the next thirty years, *why didn't I go to design school?*

I joined a religious group in place of design school. The year was 1971, and my classmates and I were excited about graduation in just a few weeks. Some kids still didn't know what they were going to do after high school, but I had known for most of the school year exactly where I was going and what I was going to be. I was less than three months away from moving out of my parent's home and into my dorm room in Pittsburg. The time to leave was so close, I could taste my new freedom and lifestyle and it was delicious. While my friends and I were planning the festivities for after the commencement, kids started showing up in school with Bibles. I heard there was a prophet speaking every night in Calvin Warner's living room. Mr. Warner was the history teacher at the high school. The rumor was, prophets were sent out by God to travel across the country on foot to preach the gospel, and one landed in Mr. Warner's living room. The Jesus Movement was happening and it came to Cattaraugus. Everyday more kids showed up in school with their Bible. The most unlikely kids were now reading the scriptures in study hall. Jim, a shy classmate who only had time for his cars, was now reading the sacred writings to the kids gathered around him. I didn't get it, but it got my curiosity. I told Jesse, my boyfriend, I wanted to go to Mr. Warner's and see what it was all about. We decided to go the next Friday night.

I was nervous about going and a little scared for my safety. I questioned whether this was a good idea. Would I be drugged and how would they drug me? *I'll make sure not to eat or drink anything while I'm there.* Would I be able to leave when I wanted to? How would they keep me? Would I be brainwashed? I knew nothing about that. Could I protect myself? I discarded all my fears and said *I'm going and I will leave when I want to.*

Jesse and I went to Mr. Warner's house and entered a packed living room. We managed to squeeze into a space on the floor farthest from where the prophet was sitting. He looked like the Jesus in portraits on living room walls. He was tall and handsome with long brown hair to his waist. He wore a burlap robe with a rope around his middle and to complete his ensemble, he wore sandals. I wasn't nervous anymore. I thought to myself, *this is going to be interesting.* I'd never been this close to a real life scam before and I couldn't believe people were buying into his act. This guy was either scamming for free food and lodging or he was just not all there. I figured a combination of both.

Once everyone arrived, the prophet started speaking. He spoke softly, not screaming the fire and brimstone I thought I was going to hear. He spoke about a loving God, someone who could truly be called my Father. He talked about how much this Father loved and cared about me. I became angry as I listened to his words. Why should I believe him? God never answered any of my prayers or helped me. I remembered back to when I was eight years old living on Long Island and pleading with God to take my life. Now, at the age of seventeen, I couldn't say I believed there was a God and I couldn't say there wasn't. I just never met him. To tell me I must have faith that there is a God, sounded like I do all the work and he does nothing. I thought *if there truly is a God then he can make his reality known, he's God, he can do anything. But to us he's invisible and we're just supposed to believe he's real.* It sounded too much like a fairytale to me.

When the prophet finished speaking, he asked if anyone would like to ask Jesus into their hearts and be saved. Right then and there I knew I was going to put God on the line. A circle was cleared for people to sit in the middle of to recite a little prayer asking God to come into their hearts and forgive them for their sins. As people went forward one at a time to recite this little prayer, I started talking to God in my mind as if he were real and listening. *"God, I'm going to sit in the circle and read the prayer. Your job is to reveal yourself to me. If you do nothing then I'll walk out of here tonight and never question again if you exist, because I'll know you don't. If you make yourself known to me then I will know you exist."*

It took about an hour before it was my turn. I went forward and sat cross-legged in the center of the circle and read the prayer. I closed my eyes and immediately I felt strong arms wrap around me. I was angry that someone was interrupting my time and angry that I was being hugged when I had such a big question on the floor for God. I tried to ignore the hug but it was hard not to feel the strong arms and tight grip. Who was doing that? I opened my eyes and looked all around. No one was in the circle with me. I closed my eyes and sat there enjoying God hugging and loving me. God showed himself to me in the best way he could have. There is no better hug than God's.

I floated home that evening in June, in the middle of the night. I actually could not feel my feet touch the ground. I entered my bedroom and heard the most beautiful music coming in through my three open windows. I put my pajamas on and jumped into bed. I stayed awake as long as I could listening to this heavenly music and fell asleep as dawn approached. When I woke up I felt someone in the room with me. I knew it was God. I asked him the question that was always on my mind.

"Why didn't you let me die when I was eight years old?"

He answered, "Because you have a message to tell."

"About what?"

"You'll know when the time is right."

I felt proud that someday I was going to have a message to tell, but most important, there was a reason for my being here. For the next seven years, God and I talked a lot to each other. I can't tell you if his voice was inside my head or outside of my body. All I know is that I heard him loud and clear.

The prophet left us after a few months and we formed a new church called Corinth.

16

Leaving Home

I loved my life walking and talking with God, but Dad was upset with my new-found faith and was doing whatever he could to stop me from going to Corinth. He said I was brainwashed and throwing my life away. He was angry that I wasn't going to school for interior design. I couldn't have cared less about decorating living rooms, kitchens, and bedrooms. God was my father now and Corinth my new family. How could I spend my days decorating when the world had so much pain and violence in it? For the first time I found peace.

I was grounded and could only leave the house for my summer job at U.S. Plywood. I moved out of my parents' home in August on my eighteenth birthday and moved in with Calvin and Alice. Soon after moving out I heard my father had a heated meeting with Calvin at Rycola Pool. Dad was threatening with his fist up, "You have to let Dody go," and took a swing at Calvin. Dad had my boss try to talk me into leaving Corinth and he even had Artie come home to show me the errors of my ways. That was the best. I was so happy to see Artie. He went to a meeting with me and got saved. He started a Bible Study as soon as he went back to his apartment on Long Island.

Dad was relentless and showed no signs of letting up. I didn't like hearing about my fathers' anger or that the buzz around town was, "What will Art White do next?" I cared for my parents and I was still trying to get my mom to like me but this did not feel good. On a Friday evening I asked God to open a door for me to be in a better place. The next morning Laurence called me from Baltimore.

I'd met Laurence at the Smithsonian in Washington on my senior class trip, and that summer Laurence and two of his friends stopped in Cattaraugus during their road trip across the country. All three of these nice young Jewish boys asked Jesus into their hearts and found their savior. They stayed in Cattaraugus for most of the summer and fellowshipped with us. On the phone Laurence said, "If you ever want to come to Baltimore, I can help you find a place to live and a job." I told him I would call him back. I didn't have a penny to my name because I had just paid Calvin for rent the night before. "God, you will have to provide." The next day, I was sitting on Calvin's front porch reading the Bible and a man stopped to look at my ten-speed bike on the sidewalk.

"Is this bike for sale?"

"Yes," and Tuesday morning I was on my seventeen-hour bus trip to Baltimore.

Jesse and I spent Sunday together discussing my trip before he drove back to school in Alfred, New York.

"I understand your wanting to get away, but why Baltimore?"

"Because that's the door God opened for me and I'm going to walk through it."

Laurence picked me up at the bus depot and we went straight to his pastor's home. Dr. Cassutto had escaped from Rotterdam Prison with the help of the guard the day before he was to be moved to Auschwitz. They both went into hiding until Hitler was destroyed. He was a short, round man with a great smile. I spent my first night in Baltimore with Dr. Cassutto and his wife, Elisabeth. They met in 1948 at a conference of Jewish Christians and were married the next year. I was intrigued to hear that Elisabeth had attended school with Anne Frank in Amsterdam.

Elisabeth's parents were captured and died in the gas chambers in Auschwitz. A Dutch woman named Grace protected and hid her until Hitler's regime was demolished.

The next day Dr. Cassutto introduced me to Ruth. She and I immediately became best friends. Ruth was going to school at Johns Hopkins to be a nurse and waitressed at Howard Johnson's Restaurant. She introduced me to her boss and I was hired on the spot. Ruth was a petite Jewish girl with long brown hair and a bubbly, charismatic personality. Her regular customers came to the restaurant and waited until a table opened up in her area. Some evenings a long line formed for those waiting to be served by Ruth. She received large tips and a nice pay at the end of each shift. I on the other hand often had empty tables and was left pennies for my tip. Needless to say, I was not a good waitress and did not feel bubbly. Ruth and I worked together, found a townhouse to rent and attended Dr. Cassutto's Emmanuel Hebrew Christian Church where he was the minister.

Jesse and I wrote often to each other and talked on the phone once a week. In November, he came to Baltimore to visit me. It was wonderful to see him. I didn't realize how much I missed him until he was standing in front of me handsome as ever. He stayed for five days and met Ruth, the people at work and attended church with us. On the morning he was leaving, he said, "Honey, let's get married. We can find an apartment in Alfred." I wanted to be with Jesse, I loved his family, and I was homesick to be closer to Cattaraugus again.

The next month we were married in a small church in Cattaraugus during a snow storm in December. Planes were late arriving at the Buffalo airport due to the storm, so we sang Christmas Carols for hours waiting for Ruth, my maid of honor to arrive from Maryland.

Jesse and I set up our new home together in a small apartment off campus in Alfred, New York, where he was going to school. I took a waitress job at the Collegiate Restaurant in town. We talked to kids about God and started a Bible Study on campus. We drove home every weekend to worship with Corinth. After Jesse graduated he accepted a job in Wellsville, New York, and I worked with a teen's group at a nearby church. In 1973 we moved back to Cattaraugus to be closer to Corinth and Jesse's family. I loved being back in my little village again. Three years later in September of 1976 our daughter Sarah Johannah Holbrook was born. We purchased our first home just before Sarah turned one. It was an adorable little white farmhouse on Main Street, complete with a big old red barn.

Corinth was changing. Two years prior to Sarah's birth, I started questioning the rules and procedures put into place. Corinth was five years old and still meeting seven days a week. Meetings started at seven in the evening and ended when they ended and never before ten. I was concerned about the children. Corinth now consisted of young families with babies and school-age kids. I strongly thought the families with kids should be able to leave early or let the moms stay home with them on school nights. Calvin's answer was always, "God will take care of them."

"Then why are they punished and reprimanded by an elder if they start squirming in their seats around nine o'clock?"

He replied, "Spare the rod, spoil the child."

I knew we were becoming thorns in Corinth's side. We were not going along with the rules and supporting everything Calvin said. Jesse and I bought a house, a car, and even a TV. These were worldly possessions and not looked upon favorably. The rules were getting stricter, our lifestyles more confining and the preaching filled with thicker damnation. It appeared that Calvin and I talked to a different God. I always listened to my God first and he hadn't changed a bit. Calvin's God didn't seem to be about love anymore. He was spending most evenings preaching about persecution. If we weren't being persecuted then we weren't doing God's work. Corinth purchased land out in the country and one evening at a meeting we discussed a mass suicide on that property. The question asked of each of us, "Would you lay down your life for God if it came to that?" Thank God, nothing ever came of that.

Calvin couldn't ask Jesse and me to leave Corinth because we were too visible in the Christian community. Jesse and I attended all the meetings at Corinth and spoke at churches, telling our stories how God came into our lives. We attended all the church revival and tent meetings with powerful evangelists. We helped transport people to the Kathryn Kuhlman healing services when ever she came to Buffalo. I was teaching in the Religious Ed after-school program and for two years I was president of the Ecumenical Society. All the churches in town and the surrounding area attended the monthly meetings I led.

I did not want Sarah brought up in this environment. When she was thirteen months old, Jesse and I asked Calvin and his wife, Alice, to stop by the house. I spoke first, "Calvin, it's wrong to make the kids sit in the nightly meetings when they have school the next day. It's wrong to reprimand them when they start squirming in their seats because they're tired. If that doesn't change, then we'll have to leave Corinth."

"Then you will have to leave Corinth."

We found out the next day that we were excommunicated and would not be recognized by members on the street. I was overwhelmed with sadness and loss. I knew we were doing the right thing, but they had been my family for seven years and now it felt like I was thrown out with the dirty garbage. Thrown out and forgotten. How could we be dismissed so easily? Every time I tried to attend a church service over the next twenty years, all I received was internal restlessness. I felt the minister was quoting scriptures to manipulate his flock. I imagined he decided what his agenda was and then used the word of God to make his point.

Eventually, I enjoyed hearing a sermon and the scriptures without experiencing an emotional trigger. Today I still do not belong to a church though I'm not opposed to it. I just haven't found one that fits me yet.

After Jesse and I left Corinth and the pain from that loss subsided, I started enjoying my newly acquired free time with Jesse's family.

17

High School Sweetheart

JESSE AND I HAD NOW BEEN MARRIED SEVEN YEARS. Void in my life growing up were grandparents, aunts, uncles, and cousins. Now I was part of a family complete with grandparents and great-grandma for our daughter Sarah. I was close to my in-laws, John and Paula, and Jesse's grandmother, Meredith, who all lived nearby. I'd known his family ever since we first moved to Cattaraugus when I was thirteen.

My mother-in-law, Paula, adored me and said I was the daughter she never had. Soon after Jesse and I married, she asked, "Dody, would you like to have a house full of beautiful furniture?"

Immediately I said, "Yes!" thinking what a great mother-in-law I have wanting to fill my house with beautiful furnishings. Not quite what I thought, but she did teach me how to strip and refinish old battered relics. Paula introduced me to country auctions. We went to many together, and I purchased furniture to refinish that I've never seen the likes of before. I bought a blanket chest because I loved its design. I had no idea what a blanket chest was but it looked beautiful in my dining room after I brought it back to life. For my birthday and holidays she always gave me a table, a chair, or something of significant age to work on for my next project. Before long I had a house full of beautiful furniture.

We enjoyed each other's company and had fun visiting antique shops on our treasure hunting trips.

I loved my father-in-law, John, just as much. He was tall, lean and looked like Norman Rockwell. He loved to write, and if it were up to him, he'd be chartering sailboats and writing novels in the Caribbean. After meeting John, it was easy to see where Jesse inherited his quick wit and dry sense of humor. I enjoyed long walks with John, and he fed me information I found interesting. Learning the same facts from another source would have been utterly boring. One cold winter day when we were out on one of our walks he explained to me the causes of frostbite and the pros and cons of cutting down your own Christmas tree. Every winter I think of frostbite and the sap in evergreens.

GG, short for great grandmother, was a strong big-boned woman ahead of her time. She didn't have to work for her liberation; it came naturally. One day I was visiting GG and she was reading a magazine article about women's sexuality.

"I don't get all the fuss about orgasms. Woman act like it's so hard to have one. When I had sex, I had an orgasm. What's the big deal? Boy, do I miss Bob. Since he died, it's the sex I miss the most." I loved that this woman in her seventies could talk so openly about everything. Like her son John, she was also a wealth of information and read books daily in her overstuffed chair.

I loved my white clapboard-sided farmhouse that had never been remodeled with the interior still boasting its original character. My kitchen was bright and sunny with an old-fashioned double door window that opened into the room over my large white porcelain sink. Lots of light came in through the double-hung window over the stove and the glass panel in the door leading to the back porch. One wall was floor to ceiling tongue-and-grove built-in cupboards that housed all our food on top and the pots and pans stored in the lower shelves. I refinished an old Hoosier cupboard for dinner dishes, glasses, silverware, and cooking utensils.

One afternoon while washing the dishes with my window wide open, I stood still and quietly watched a deer eat from my apple tree just ten feet away. For the first time in my life I experienced happy butterflies in my stomach. I felt pure contentment and a connection with nature and my world.

I didn't work outside the home, so that gave me a lot of time to work inside. I pulled up all the linoleum and carpets in the house and sanded the wood floors before sealing them with a satin finish. I tore down the old wallpaper and repapered all the rooms. Every window and interior door frame received a fresh coat of white paint along with our seven-inch-tall baseboards. I went to auctions and brought home treasures for restoring to keep with the style of my old farmhouse. Once a week I baked homemade bread following a recipe as old as our homestead. I took a quilt-making class and created quilts, throws, pillows, and placemats with matching napkins and sold my works of art at a boutique located inside of Hengerer's Department Store in downtown Buffalo, New York.

Lynn was my best friend and I loved our time together. Amy, a mutual friend of ours introduced us to each other. Amy and her family were moving back to Mississippi and she had a long to-do list of things to accomplish before the move. Introducing Lynn and me to each other was on her list. After months of conflicting schedules, we finally got together in Amy's kitchen just before she left. Lynn and I immediately connected as Amy knew we would.

Lynn had a son near Sarah's age and it didn't take long before the four of us spent most of our free time together. During the summer months we played with the kids at Rycola Pool. Year round we took long walks in Lynn's apple orchard out in the country. She was captivated by her land and loved describing her dream house built on it. She pretended to be walking from room to room and acted out opening a window overlooking the picturesque countryside. We worked on our crafts and signed up for local bazaars when we accumulated enough inventory. One of our many projects was organizing an aerobics class. She taught the class and I carried out the routines alongside her as her assistant. Lynn and I worked well together, sharing the same level of energy. We were two young women who never stopped.

Jesse was a draftsman at U.S. Plywood and came home for lunch everyday. Often we made plans for trips to take with Sarah. I loved our picnics at Niagara Falls in Canada and exploring Allegany State Park near Pennsylvania. Toronto was my favorite destination for weekends away.

I was happy but still overshadowed by not feeling normal and still trying to hide it. Happy, Depression and Rage wrestled inside of me constantly. Happy did not visit often but I was aware that she existed. I was very familiar with Depression throughout my life and I was good at hiding her. She never stayed long and I didn't understand why she had to come at all. How could I be happy one moment and then with my next breath be hit with a huge wave of depression? I never received a warning she was coming or how long she would stay, and I never knew where she came from or why. I kept to myself when Depression came. Being quiet and reading helped get me through it.

Rage on the other hand was not easy to deal with. I didn't meet Rage until after Jesse and I married. I was a woman out of control when she surfaced and showed her ugly face. I screamed at my husband, I threw furniture and broke walls. Too bad I couldn't tear down my internal emotionally scarred walls instead of our lath and plaster ones. My husband became the root of all my pain. I believed that Jesse did not love me, was not proud of me and didn't think of me as a significant person in his life. Jesse had his own agenda to follow and I believed it didn't include me. He was always where I wasn't. If I was inside, he was out. If I was reading a book in the living room, he was paging through a magazine in the family room. In place of sitting on the sofa together, we had our own separate chairs. Jesse was a quiet man and it was hard to engage him into a conversation. I longed for touch, but he was not a touchy-feely guy. I ached for him to put his arm around me or to hold my hand. The lack of communication, touch, and support I so wanted and didn't receive opened the door for Rage. I learned many years later the recipe that made up our marriage created an emotional trigger in me. I mistook Jesse's behavior and busyness as wanting to be away from me. His quietness meant he didn't care about me or was interested in anything I was doing. I accepted his lack of touch to mean, "I don't love you." When Rage surfaced, I was overwhelmed with thoughts like, "It's not supposed to be like this. Where's my husband that adores me and loves living with me?" I didn't know at the time, I was actually feeling the rejection from my parents, mostly my mother. Rage didn't surface because of anger at Jesse. I felt Rage because I was angry at my mom for not liking me, for not comforting me or protecting me. I was angry at Mom for never putting her arm around me or being proud of something I accomplished. I was angry at her for locking me in closets and killing my pets and breaking my toys. I was not aware of my anger towards my mother, but it was there, so it came out at Jesse. The feelings I had were real but they were transferred onto the wrong person.

Why did I marry Jesse? I wanted my own family. I loved his family and I wanted to be part of their normal lifestyle. I couldn't have picked a better family. The problem was, I was not ready to live a normal life.

I couldn't eat without physical pain, so I ate as little as possible, enough to stay alive and not enough to hurt. I bordered on anorexia most of my adult life. On one occasion I experienced my whole body out of control and I was losing two pounds a day. The nausea was fierce, I couldn't eat without vomiting. When I weighed in at seventy-five pounds I called Lynn and asked her to take me to my doctor. He was not pleased when I walked into his exam room. His voice was loud and stern, "Why are you doing this to yourself? Why do you want to die?"

"I'm not anorexic. I don't want to lose weight and I'm here because I want to live."

After he calmed down, he gave me Inderal to slow my heart and said, "I don't know what's going on in your life to trigger such an episode but whatever it is you need to change it."

I didn't want to end my marriage, but I didn't know how to stay in it. If my self-esteem was on the ground floor when Jesse and I married, it was now in the basement. We were part of Corinth for the first seven years of our marriage and I was the subservient wife. Jesse made all the major decisions for our family and controlled the money. It was next to impossible to acquire any spending money, which was why I sold my quilted items in Buffalo. I asked Jesse in our eighth year of marriage, "When did clothes shopping become a luxury?"

A few weeks after I returned from seeing my doctor about my racing heart, I entered the living room on a Sunday evening around eight o'clock, sat down and said to Jesse, "Honey, I haven't been very happy in this marriage and I don't know if I ever will be. I feel distrustful and crazy and my body hurts all the time. I think we should look at divorce." He stood up, looked at me for a second and walked out the back door without ever saying a word. He was gone for twenty-four hours. Monday evening he walked into the house at eight o'clock, sat in his chair and said, "Make an appointment with Mr. Berry." I made the appointment and Jesse and I went to see Lynn's father who was the attorney in town. He suggested we do a year separation because after twelve months it can be canceled and the marriage continues or it automatically turns into a divorce. We filed for the separation.

My brothers Bill and Bob came to help load the truck on moving day. I woke up that morning and started to walk across my empty bedroom. The floor felt like it was moving in large waves. I didn't know what was happening. I was seasick from the floor heaving and the psychedelic colors added to my dizziness. It looked like Northern Lights in my bedroom. I cried. I didn't want to leave my husband, who I loved, and the guilt at the thought of Sarah and her father not living together was overwhelming. I didn't want to leave my in-laws, or my farmhouse. I got down on the floor and crawled slowly to the phone. I called Lynn. I thought she would tell me to stay because she didn't believe in divorce. But, she didn't give me the comforting words I was looking for. She told me I was panicking and having an anxiety attack and to continue with the move. She said, "Dody, Jesse loves you and if you want to come back in two weeks, you know he will take you back with open arms. Just give it two weeks."

When the truck was loaded, my brothers left for their homes, and Jesse, Sarah, and I drove away to Sarah's and my new apartment in Ellicottville, New York, fifteen miles away. Jesse stayed with us for a few days while we settled into our new home. It was hard to say good-bye. We were both fearful of our future without the other one in it. We also knew that it was too confusing for Sarah, so Jesse went back to the house in Cattaraugus, now empty of furniture. We had been married for ten years and Sarah was four at the time of our separation.

For the last three years of our marriage Depression and Rage were making regular visits and I didn't want to feel depressed or angry anymore and I thought I had to leave the marriage to fix my life.

At the end of two weeks my body was calm and relaxed and I felt wonderful. I felt in control of my life again, another plus. I was okay. I didn't realize until I left the marriage how controlling Jesse was. I was a subservient wife with no voice. I missed Cattaraugus, but I was excited and hopeful about Sarah's and my future. It took Sarah longer to adjust to her new life away from her dad, her home, her grandparents, GG, and Cattaraugus.

18

Father Knows Best

SARAH WAS NOT DOING WELL IN OUR NEW LIFE away from her father and family in Cattaraugus. She cried out her pain in anger, "I hate it here. I want my daddy and I want all this stuff back in our house with Daddy. He doesn't have anything and he needs me." She cried herself to sleep every night. I was sad over my daughter's pain and the changes she had to make. Not only had she lost all that was familiar to her, she also lost me during the day. I had to work full time and she had to go to daycare. Mary, who owned the daycare, said she couldn't have Sarah any longer. After two weeks she was still crying throughout the day, and it was upsetting the other children. She tried everything to make it work but ran out of ideas.

Sarah and I went to visit my mother, who I was still trying to get to like me. I told her about Sarah having a tough time adjusting to her new life and asked if she would watch Sarah during the day. It seemed like a good idea because Sarah was familiar with her grandma Marilyn and maybe this would be an opportunity for us to get close. I no longer had Paula as my mother-in-law, maybe Mom and I could have a mother-daughter relationship. She said yes and I found an apartment a few blocks from her home in Eden, New York, a suburb of Buffalo. I enjoyed seeing my mother a couple times a day and Sarah didn't cry as much. My biggest challenge was bedtime. She wanted to sleep in my bed, and I thought that would open the door for other problems. Looking back, why didn't I let her? I could have slept in her bed or on the sofa. Was it wrong for her to sleep with me? Why didn't I ask for help or find answers to my questions? My daughter was in pain and I didn't know how to comfort her.

On a Friday evening after Jesse picked Sarah up for his weekend with her, my friend Rhonda and I went to a nightclub in Buffalo. Once we arrived, Rhonda, who was a man magnet, disappeared immediately. She would be busy picking and choosing all night long. As much as I looked like the girl next door with my long brown hair and fresh looking face, Rhonda looked like the other woman. Her body was drop dead gorgeous and men were drawn to her like flies to spilled pop.

I listened to the music as I stood at a tall table sipping my safe drink Gin and Tonic. I hated Gin and Tonic, so one lasted all evening. I came to dance, not to drink. I felt a tap on my shoulder and was pleased when I turned to view a tall man dressed in a black shirt with gray slacks looking masculine with a hint of adorableness with his curly salt-and-pepper hair. We walked onto the dance floor together and fell into a compatible rhythm. When the band stopped to take a break, so did we, and Jason introduced himself. He had as much charisma as he did good looks, and I was attracted to him immediately. I soon learned that everyone loved Jason. He was outgoing, friendly and from Pennsylvania. Whoever came up with the slogan for their license plate, "You've got a friend in Pennsylvania," knew Jason. It was obscene the number of friends he had.

Soon into our conversation he started talking about his sons and whipped out his wallet showing me pictures of his three boys. Blair, age thirteen, was the rocket scientist in the family and rarely seen without a book in hand. Daniel, age twelve, equally bright, was always accompanied by a hockey stick or football, and the youngest, Ethan, age seven, was still having a tough time since his mom left. Jason and I danced until the club closed and then he and his friend and Rhonda and I walked next door for breakfast. I was sitting in the booth watching Jason return from the men's room thinking *My, he sure is handsome.* It was a powerful handsome not like James Bond, 007, more like the Godfather, ready to close the deal or have someone killed. Although Jason looked like he was straight out of the mafia, it was "Father Knows Best" that surfaced when he spoke. After breakfast he walked me over to my car and asked, "Do you have plans for Sunday?"

"No, my ex is bringing my daughter back in the morning."

"My boys will be coming home Sunday evening after spending two weeks at their grandparents' place in Pennsylvania. Why don't you and your daughter drive up in the afternoon and we'll have a picnic on the beach."

"I'd love to, that sounds wonderful."

On Sunday, Sarah and I drove to Jason's house in Hamburg near Buffalo. On the ride up she talked all about her weekend in Cattaraugus. She played with her best friend, Mandy, who was five days older than Sarah. Jesse and I met Mandy's parents at our Lamaze class. Sarah's spirits were up and it did my heart good to see her happy and talkative. We arrived at Jason's and after the introductions he drove us to the beach ten minutes away. His charisma put Sarah right at ease and she was comfortable with him.

Jason ran thirty feet down the beach, fell to his knees and yelled, "Sarah, come see what I found." We couldn't stop laughing watching her run towards him. Her little legs working hard trying to capture sound footing in the sand looked like she was running in slow motion. Jason kept running away from her and she kept chasing him. Each time he dropped to his knees he scooped up a new little treasure and every time she was mesmerized by the tiny shell to add to their collection.

After a day of collecting shells and driftwood, we headed back to Jason's house. His parents had dropped the boys off and headed back to Pennsylvania while we were at the beach. Jason introduced his sons to Sarah and me. Each one was fighting for the floor to talk. After being gone for two weeks, they had a lot to tell. Sarah and I looked at each other as if to say, *have you ever seen and heard so much excitement before and so loud?* We enjoyed watching their flurry of enthusiasm and I loved how relaxed they were with their dad.

Daniel, his head in the freezer said, "Dad, can I have . . ."

"Don't you dare touch that. Blair help your brother put plates, forks, and napkins on the table."

Jason grabbed the box from the freezer, took a cake out and started singing Happy Birthday with the boys and Sarah joining in. Sometime Friday evening at the club I mentioned it was my birthday. Our friendship was off to a nice start.

We went dancing a few more times and to Niagara Falls for picnics with the kids. He was the first man to join me at the theater to see a kid's movie. He loved that stuff.

One evening mid-week Jason called to invite me to a football game at Rich Stadium, the Bills were playing the Steelers. I told him I had plans on Sunday and wouldn't be able to.

"Do you have plans with family?"

"No."

"Are you committed to it? Can you cancel?"

"Jason, let's go to the next home game together."

"Do you have a date?"

"Yes." But I didn't tell him I was going to see the Bills play the Steelers with the manager from the tire shop I'd met last Saturday.

I heard an icy cold, "FINE," and he hung up. My first "red flag" dating Jason just waved in front of me. It was two weeks before he called again. I missed him and the boys and I was happy to hear his voice.

"May I come over tonight?"

"Sure."

Sarah answered the door. "Jason!" She threw her arms around him. "Come see my pictures. Grandma has lots of coloring books and crayons and stickers too." After a few hours and bedtime arriving too soon for Sarah, who wasn't done entertaining Jason, it was a struggle keeping her in bed. Finally she fell asleep and it was our time to talk.

"Dody, I missed you a lot. I was surprised at how much I missed you. I'm not very good at this dating stuff. I do all right in the beginning, but eventually I stop trusting the women I'm dating."

"Maybe in time it'll get easier."

"Well, I have to leave now."

That was weird. I was hoping he came over to apologize for hanging up on me so we could move forward in our dating again. That didn't happen.

Two weeks later Jason called, "Hi, can we try this again. I don't blame you if you say no, but I would love to take you out to dinner Saturday evening."

"It's a date. I look forward to seeing you Jason."

We ate at The Hamburg Station. Great food, nice ambiance, and the restaurant was actually built into the side of a real caboose. We talked about Blair, Daniel, Ethan, and Sarah throughout dinner and dessert. Our conversation turned serious when we got back to my place.

"Dody, can I tell you about the time Noreen left?"

"Yes."

"It wasn't just her leaving, it was also the way she left. It was a Sunday morning and it was Blair's birthday. She asked me to take the boys to Buffalo to visit a friend while she prepared the house for his party. We came home after a few hours and entered into a quiet house void of decorations and cake. I ran upstairs and opened the closet door to find all her clothes gone. No note and no warning that she was planning to leave. Devastation and depression entered our home that day with tsunami force. We were a mess for quite a while and Ethan still is. We cried a lot at first, and Blair kept asking, "What did I do?" Daniel stopped talking and played street hockey twenty-four/seven. Ethan cried a lot and kept asking when his mother was coming home. I obtained full custody of the boys when we hit the one-year mark of her disappearance. I had no idea she was so unhappy in our marriage. I can't believe I was so stupid and didn't see it coming."

I fell in love with this man who hurt so deeply and shared his feelings with me. I loved being near his unwavering strength of character and I entertained the thought that Sarah and I might be a family with him and his boys one day. We spent a lot of time at his place because it was larger and he had more kids. Going to Jason's meant we were going to laugh and have fun. He was always picking Sarah up and swinging her in the air and wrestling with her on the floor. He's the only man who'd ever played with her and she loved it. As our relationship grew stronger, Sarah's bedtime problems vanished.

Jason called me one day at the courthouse in Little Valley, New York where I was doing title search work and asked if he could stop by my place after work. He was waiting for me in the driveway when I pulled in.

"Hi, honey," I said.

He didn't answer.

We walked upstairs to my second floor apartment. We sat down at the kitchen table and he cradled my hands in his.

"What's wrong?"

"I don't know how to say this."

"Noreen came back didn't she?"

"Yes."

"That's a good thing. Have the boys seen her yet?"

"She's coming over tomorrow to talk to them."

"That's good. You've all waited a long time for this day."

"Noreen and I talked."

The minute I heard "Noreen and I" it hit me that there might be a Noreen and Jason again. I hid my feelings and pretended to be strong, "Do you think you'll get back together?"

"I don't know."

"But you're open to it?"

"I don't know, we were married for sixteen years and we have three boys together. I don't know what will happen. I'm sorry. I hate to do this to you."

At that very moment all I could think was, *If you love something, let it go. If it comes back, it's yours. If it doesn't, it never was.* I hugged him, "Honey, I love you and I know you need to do what you need to do."

In the middle of Noreen's Homecoming sat two people in love with each other. I was happy that she returned but I was not anticipating the hardball thrown straight into my stomach when she did. Finding out that the man I loved wanted the woman who destroyed his life in enormous proportions instead of me opened up my own wounds. *I can't do this dating thing anymore. How many times can I fall in love and have it not work before it destroys me completely?*

I went to my mother's to pick Sarah up and stayed for dinner. I tried to explain to Sarah about the boy's mother coming back into their lives and how they all needed to talk about whether or not they could be a family again. This was pretty big stuff to try to explain to a four-year-old. Both Sarah and I were sad again. She stopped talking and smiling and I tried to act like I was okay most of the time. Sometimes we cried together and bedtime became a problem again, only this time, for both of us.

After a month Jason came over when Sarah was at her father's for the weekend in Cattaraugus.

"How are the boys?"

"Good."

"How are you?"

"Okay."

"How are you and Noreen?"

"There is no me and Noreen. She never wanted to get back together. She showed up because she wanted a divorce and needed me to sign the papers."

"Oh."

"It hurt again, but not like when she left the first time. Eventually I realized it wouldn't have worked. I could never trust her again. I needed to figure out if I could ever trust anyone again. I kept coming back to you and Sarah and how much I missed you two and wanted us all to be a family together. I love you guys."

We spent the rest of the afternoon laughing and hugging and we couldn't wait to tell the kids we were back together. I was proud of myself for surviving that breakup and glad Jason had the time to figure out his feelings and put closure to his relationship with Noreen. We were married a year later. I was twenty-nine and he was ten years older.

19

The Trucker

SOON AFTER WE MARRIED, JASON ASKED his sons if they wanted to call me Mom. All three said, "Yes." Sarah said, "If the boys get to call you Mom, can I call Jason, Daddy?" We had to think about that one. The boy's mother, although she was back in the area, rarely saw them and was not very interested in their lives. Sarah's father only lived an hour away and she saw him regularly. I said to Sarah, "You have two dads, I don't see why you can't call Jason Daddy."

"What's my dad's name in Cattaraugus?"

"Jesse."

I'll Call Jason, Daddy, and I'll call my other dad, Daddy Jesse."

We were a family and I loved our family. I was happy most of the time. How could I not be? I had this great man . . . well I knew he wasn't that great. He was controlling and liked to have his own way. I was okay with that. I still didn't know what my own way was. He showed signs of jealousy from time to time. So what? I loved telling him how much I loved him. Whenever he did something that upset me, I just thought about our last picnic with the kids and my frown turned upside down. I wasn't naive, I could see that another woman might not put up with the same stuff I was capable of living with. Jason gave me everything I wanted, he loved our kids and the family came first.

Rage rarely surfaced. Happy stayed with me for long periods and Depression snuck in every so often out of the blue with no warning as usual. I still hid her when she came and ignored her presence the best I could. Jason was on the road a lot and the kids were all busy with each other and their friends in the neighborhood, so it was easy for me to lose myself in my books while Depression visited. The most important thing I learned about Depression when she visited me was I knew her days were short and Happy would return soon.

Jason asked me one day if he could adopt Sarah. I asked Jesse and he said, "No." Jason loved having a little girl in the house and the boys loved having a sister. They all took on the job of protecting her whenever she ventured outside to play. One day Ethan came running into the house out of breath, "Mom, you have to see Sarah in the park." I couldn't tell if I was going to find something I liked seeing or not. I tore out of the house as fast as I could and ran to the park four doors away. Daniel was holding the arms of a nine-year-old boy pinned behind his back while five-year-old Sarah threw punches into his stomach.

"That's enough, stop. Why are you doing that?"

Sarah stopped punching the boy while Daniel wouldn't let go of the boys arms and said, "This bully told Sarah she wasn't allowed in the park and she came and told me. I walked back here with her and told him, 'Nobody tells my sister she can't play in the park.' And I held him while Sarah punched him."

"We're not going to have anymore bullying or punching. The park belongs to everyone and please let me know if a problem happens again. It's time to come home. Dinner is almost ready."

While we walked to the house and for the rest of the evening, it was all about Sarah. "Wow! Sarah you can really punch. You've got a strong right arm. Dad, you should have seen Sarah beat up a bully twice her size in the park today. He's never going to mess with her again."

Sarah couldn't stop beaming. She loved the affirmations her brothers showered on her. She received a huge dose of self-esteem that day even though it came from an episode of physical force. I loved seeing her radiant spirit and I couldn't have been happier for her.

I didn't work the first year of our marriage. I thought it was a good plan to stay home and help everyone get acclimated to our new family. The boys needed a break from taking care of the house and experience the freedom of being kids again. We played a lot that first year. During warm weather we divided our time between picnics at Niagara Falls and the beach on Lake Erie. During the winter months we went sledding and to games at Rich Stadium when the Bills were home. We hosted the neighborhood football parties when they were away.

The time came when I had to go back to work. My favorite part about entering the work force again was coming home at the end of each day. I loved not being able to get through the front door because the three boys and Sarah were so excited to tell me about their day. Jason always had to say, "Move back. Let Mom come in," and we all laughed at what a spectacle we were and how good we felt together.

I was up early one morning getting Sarah and Ethan ready for school. After I watched them leave on their school bus I went back to bed for a short nap. I woke up hearing the front door slam, and Jason running up the stairs, then pounding on the bedroom door, yelling, "Unlock the door!"

I answered back, "The door isn't locked."

He kept pounding and yelling, "Unlock the door!"

"Okay, I'm getting up."

He continued pounding and yelling, "Unlock the door." I opened the door. It wasn't locked, and Jason wasn't there. My heart started pounding and I slowly walked down the stairs. No one was in the house. I looked at the kitchen clock, it was 8:15. That was the time Blair and Daniel left for school each morning. It wasn't Jason entering the house that woke me up, it must have been Blair and Daniel leaving and the door slamming behind them.

Hearing someone speak to me who wasn't there and answering back scared me. I remembered my friend Christine next door telling me how much she liked their marriage counselor so I asked her for his phone number. I called Dr. Zoar and told him about the Unlock the Door conversation and what he thought had happened. He said, "I think I have someone for you to tell that to. May I call you back tomorrow?"

"Yes, thank you."

Dr. Zoar called the next day, "I spoke with Barbara Mitchell and I want you to call her and tell her what you told me. Barbara is very good and she will help you to understand what occurred."

I called Barbara Mitchell and made an appointment. After I told her about the 'Unlock the Door' conversation, she said, "I have an assignment for you. When you have some quiet time for yourself, I want you to write down your first memory. Next, write something about each year after that. It doesn't have to be long, just something from each year."

That evening I was prepared to write. Jason was a truck driver and his schedule was on the road for two weeks and then home for two weeks. He was on the road at the time. It was late and the kids were all in bed. My writing tablet was on my lap, pen in hand and I started thinking. I wrote about the house in St. Louis, how I ran out the front door barefoot and got stung by a bee when I was four, fishing on the bank of a creek with Artie at five, moving to Long Island and starting my new kindergarten class. At six I thought about first grade and learning to read. At seven, I remembered my teacher and playing with friends on the playground.

I moved onto third grade and I saw the chalkboard and the cursive letters above it. My head started pounding and my stomach cramping. The more I tried to think about being eight, the more my stomach hurt until I fell off the sofa onto the floor doubled over in pain. As I lay on the floor, my mind would not let me think about eight, so I tried nine. Same thing, no memory and the pain persisted. I tried to think of something at ten, nothing, still more pain. I'm not convinced yet that there was a connection between my pain and trying to think about those years, but I was thinking that I should call for Blair to get an ambulance. The pain was excruciating, but when I thought of something at age eleven, the pain subsided. I had no trouble remembering something from all my other years. Ten minutes after leaving the age of ten the pain was completely gone. One last time I tried to go back to those three missing years and the pain started again. I ended the assignment.

In my second visit with Barbara, I told her about the pain and the missing years. She explained to me how our brain protects us from situations that may be too large to handle at the time and won't surface until we can face the trauma that occurred. Barbara said, "Unlock the Door is your subconscious telling you it's time to unlock the memories of those missing years. Your next assignment is to go and ask your family what they remember about those years and about you during that time."

I asked Dad, and he got a big fat headache and said, "I don't remember those years either." I asked Kathy and she said, "I don't remember anything about you, I was too busy taking care of Billy and Bobby." I asked Artie, "Yeah, I remember you during that time. I was worried. You changed overnight. You became this little hood. You wore nothing but black and you were tough. You were different, not you. I kept telling Mom, there's something wrong with Dody, and she just ignored me. Why, what was going on?"

"I don't know, I have no memory of those years. I wore black and I was a little hood?" I couldn't picture myself being tough.

I asked Mom, and she said, "Mr. Stewart was your teacher in the third grade and you didn't do any school work that year. You were tested to see if you needed to repeat third grade and we were ordered to take you to a doctor for three sessions to be evaluated. You completed third and fourth grade in the next school year."

"What did the doctor tell you after my third visit?"

"He said if you didn't get help, you would go into La La Land."

"Mom, I did go into La La Land. I have no memory of the next three years after I stopped seeing the doctor."

The scene that happened next was the scariest display of my mother's rage I'd ever witnessed. She started screaming at the top of her lungs, "I WON'T REMEMBER THAT TIME AND YOU CAN'T MAKE ME REMEMBER." All the while she was screaming, she was pounding her fists on the table and jumping up and down. She looked like a rabid, wild animal.

Soon after I brought up those missing years, my mother harmed my daughter. Sarah was five years old and spending the afternoon with Grandma. When they arrived at our house, Sarah came through the front door, out of breath with tears streaming down her face, "Grandma hurt me. Grandma hurt me."

My mother walked in behind her. "I have no idea what she's talking about. All of a sudden, out of the blue, she started screaming. I think there's something very wrong with your daughter."

Sarah shouted at her grandma, "You hurt me on purpose. You saw my leg wasn't inside the car and you shut the door on it anyway."

I pulled Sarah close to me and wrapped my arms tight around her and told my mother to leave. While giving me the evil eye, she said, "You spoil that child. She's got you wrapped around her little finger. You'll believe anything she says."

"That's right Mom, I will." After my mother left, I looked at Sarah's leg. It was already black and blue and the skin was cut where the door slammed on her. I suffered huge consequences bringing up those missing years to my mother and the worse one was my daughter getting hurt.

Soon after my mother and I parted, Jason started withdrawing from me. When I asked him what was wrong, he ignored me. When I asked, "Why did we stop doing things together and as a family?" his anger was not the answer I was looking for.

"Won't you ever be happy? I can't do enough for you can I? I'm gone two weeks at a time working my ass off for this family and it's still not enough. Do you think I like being on the road, sleeping in the back of my truck, not seeing my kids? You're crazy. Go talk to one of your imaginary people and leave me alone."

I was alone. My mother was never going to like me and my husband pulled away. *When did he stop loving me? Does he think I'm crazy? Does he want to end the marriage? If I only knew how to approach him, but how could I, he's rarely home and when he is, he acts like I'm not.*

My friend Shelley lived across the street. She was my age, divorced and had a daughter Sarah's age. We spent a lot of time at each other's home sharing coffee and books. One evening I was at Shelley's looking through her books and picked up *Sybil*. I always wanted to read it but never did. I was pretty sure Sybil and I suffered from the same sickness and I didn't want it confirmed. That evening I was curious enough to bring the book home. Once I started reading it, I couldn't put it down. By the time I finished it, I thought it might be possible that I was schizophrenic, but I didn't think I had it as bad as Sybil. Maybe I only had a few people pulling for me internally. And I hoped that I would never act out as badly as Sybil had. That thought scared me. For sure I would be put away if I was found in the middle of a fountain talking to imaginary people. Barbara didn't think I was crazy, but maybe she would have found out I was if I had kept on seeing her.

Saturday morning I walked over to Shelley's for a cup of coffee and to return her book and she asked how I liked it. "I found it interesting."

"This weekend is a Sybil marathon. This afternoon is part one and tomorrow is part two."

"Great! It'll be fun to see the movie right after reading the book."

I was enthralled with the movie that I thought I had watched that weekend, but I would not understand until fifteen years later why it took me ten times to watch Sybil before I felt I had seen the whole movie. Every time I played it, I discovered new scenes I hadn't seen before.

20

Can It Get Any Worse

WITHIN A YEAR OF BRINGING UP my three missing childhood years to my mother, the doorbell rang. I was served divorce papers. It was just before Christmas and Jason took the boys to Pennsylvania to spend a month with his parents over the holidays. By now, he looked at me with contempt and I didn't have a clue why.

I immediately found an apartment for Sarah and me. What else could I do? My husband wanted a divorce. I didn't want to be with someone who didn't love me. That was too much like living in the home I grew up in. Sarah and I moved out before Jason and the boys returned from Pennsylvania.

Jason called one day, "Today our divorce is final, will you meet me for a drink?"

"Yes." My neighbor upstairs watched Sarah while I walked to the neighborhood pub to meet him.

I spoke first after we sat down, "Why did you want a divorce?"

"Because your mother told me you were having affairs when I was on the road."

"Why didn't you tell me she was saying that?"

"You'd only deny it. I believed your mother. Why would a mother make up a story like that about her daughter if it wasn't true?"

98

"Jason, it wasn't true. I can't believe you didn't talk to me about it. This is crazy, I need to leave."

"Can I bring the boys over tomorrow to see you and Sarah?"

"Yeah, Sarah needs to see you and the boys, and we need to figure out how to explain to them why all our lives just got turned upside down."

The next day he brought the boys over, and while they went for a walk with Sarah, Jason and I talked about dating or getting married again. I ended it after a few dates, "Jason, this isn't going to work. You have trust issues and now I have trust issues. I'm still angry that you never told me what my mother was saying to you about me and I'm angry that you believed her instead of talking to me. We both brought our dysfunctional luggage into this marriage and we were still good together. We were happy, our kids were happy and I never would have cheated on you, but I don't ever want to live through your pulling away from me again. Now I know I'm powerless to bring you back." We never explained to the kids why we ended.

My mother knew Jason was vulnerable and just what buttons to push. She accomplished what she'd set out to do and my marriage ended. *Why did she hate me so much?*

Once again our lives were turned upside down and Sarah and I were facing another new beginning. The joy and happiness that had been in her life for the last three and a half years had now disappeared. She looked like a little walking zombie, quiet and lifeless. She wouldn't talk, hardly ate, didn't play, and sat at the end of the sofa curled up staring at the TV. How could I tell her that,with time, it would get better? Sarah withdrew and I went into denial for reasons I'm not sure of. Was I afraid to see my daughter's pain or was my own pain too big? I needed to stay present to raise my daughter and I had to work—a nervous breakdown was not an option. I wanted to die, but that wasn't an option either. Why didn't I get help for us?

Friday evening Jesse came to pick up Sarah for his weekend with her and she started crying and yelling, "I won't go." The whole time she was holding onto one of the four posters of her bed and Jesse was trying to peel her off. After playing tug-a-war with Sarah and the bed for forty-five minutes, he said, "I can't take her like this. If she wants to stay that bad, she should."

After Jesse left and Sarah fell asleep, I walked into the kitchen to make a cup of tea and stood frozen in the middle of the room. I couldn't move my arms or legs. I wanted to yell, but I couldn't make a sound. I was terrified that I might be having a heart attack. Slowly, feeling started coming back and I prayed, "God, please open a door for me to be someplace else, I need to be away from here." The next morning Artie called and said, "Dody, I need a bookkeeper for the magazine. The job is yours if you want it and we have a place for you and Sarah to stay." I started making plans to move to Massachusetts.

21

The Engineer

BILL AND BOB DROVE THE U-HAUL TRUCK carrying our worldly possessions while I drove the car packed full of every sad emotion a person was capable of feeling. Sarah cried the entire way from Buffalo to Massachusetts minus one hour when sleep gave her a short reprieve from her pain. She was still grieving the loss of Jason and the boys and here we were moving again. How many times could her spirit be crushed? How much heartache could an eight-year-old take? Everything she loved was taken away from her. How much loss could she survive before she stopped caring all together?

Jesse gave me written permission to leave the state of New York with Sarah and had one request, "If you marry again, can Sarah call me Daddy instead of Daddy Jesse?"

We moved to Otis, Massachusetts, high on a hill in the Berkshires with breathtaking views of the rolling countryside. We settled into the homestead where Artie's wife, Bess, grew up. Her father ran a summer camp and tree farm on the property that consisted of three large buildings plus a variety of barns. A stately two-story Georgian style home was where Bess's parents, George and Carol, lived. A one-story ranch was connected to the main house by a breezeway where Artie, Bess, and their newborn son,

Evan, lived. The bunkhouse resembled a two-story stable that Sarah and I would soon call home. On the second floor of the bunkhouse were two large rooms where the kids slept during summer camp, one for the boys and one for the girls. On the tour of our new home, we peeked into the two massive bathrooms complete with a long row of sinks, shower stalls, and toilets, one for the boys and the other for the girls. Sarah and I slept in a large private room that housed the only bed with a mattress on it.

Our life was finally slowing down to a nice pace with a regular routine. Sarah and I gathered eggs daily from the chicken coop and visited the cows on our way back to the main house. We always stopped to talk to them. Cows are great creatures to work out life's problems with. Their ears perk up and they look so intently at you as if they are giving you their undivided attention as you share your story with them. I'd been talking to cows for years. To this day, Sarah still has a fondness for cows. At night, we lay in bed with our windows wide open and listened to the coyotes howling.

"How far away are they?"

"The coyotes?"

"Yea."

"I don't think very far. I'm sure they live in the woods nearby."

"I miss Jason and the boys."

"I know, honey."

"Will I ever see them again?"

"I hope so. We can call them, you know."

"I know, but everything is different now."

Sarah and I shared the big bed together and every night she fell asleep while talking. I was happy Sarah was able to fall asleep.

I loved being near Artie again and Bess was a sensitive, kind sister-in-law. She was easy to be around and I liked her. In time Sarah's mood started to improve as she experienced the benefits of knowing her Uncle Artie. He was still a clown and helped her find laughter again.

In the fall Sarah started third grade in a new school in Lee, Massachusetts. I felt it was time to move out of the bunkhouse and have our own place with two bedrooms, a kitchen, a living room, and a small bathroom with one sink, one tub, and one toilet, a welcomed change to our large bath that accommodated twelve people at a time. I found an apartment across the street from Sarah's school and a daycare next door.

At the same time Sarah and I were moving to Lee, Artie and Bess decided to close down the magazine and open an advertising agency. I found a job at E. Caligari and Son in Great Barrington, Massachusetts. I answered their ad in the classifieds for an Interior Decorator Apprentice. I was excited about the prospects of this job and met with the owner, Bill Caligari, and Sonny the interior decorator. Bill was a tall, handsome man that could have passed for Charlton Heston's twin brother. He also had the same passionate, friendly demeanor that Charlton played in so many of his movies. Sonny was the exact opposite. He was a high-spirited, lean man that moved as fast as his words. He didn't just say "carpet," he flew to the carpets to show me what he was describing. My head spun watching him move throughout the store. Sonny welcomed me into his decorating world with excited approval. My spirit did jumping jacks at the anticipation of my new career.

The interview went well and Mr. Caligari offered me the apprentice position. He said, "Sonny thinks you'll be perfect, and it's important that he can work well with the person I hire because he'll be training you in all the areas of decorating. I'm also going to offer you the bookkeeping position we have open because your resume shows you are qualified for that job as well, it's your choice."

"What position would you like to fill first?"

"The bookkeeper."

"Then I'll take the bookkeeper position."

What was so seriously wrong with me that I still couldn't ask for what I wanted?

Artie watched Sarah and Evan every Friday evening at our apartment while Bess and I anticipated taking in some serious dancing. He was happy she finally had someone to dance with and enjoyed movie night with Sarah who loved Friday nights with her Uncle Artie, watching special flicks he picked out and eating popcorn. It was the highlight of her week. Evan was content spending his Friday evenings sleeping nearby with the occasional bottle and diaper change.

When Bess and I first ventured out on our Friday nights, our plan was to visit a new club each week until we found our favorite spot. This was easier said than done. The Berkshires seemed to be in a slump and suffering from a loss of night life. We were frustrated during our first few weeks of not finding one place to dance let alone our favorite place. Some establishments advertised dancing. We went only to find out they'd eliminated the dancing part. During the week we asked people, "Where's a good place to go dancing." Word of mouth was not a good source either. Friday nights we drove to places that were highly recommended only to find they had closed down. One Friday evening, Bess, Artie, and Evan showed up at the apartment, and Bess beamed with excitement over stumbling onto a real live lead during the week.

"Dody, I was on Route 183 between Stockbridge and Great Barrington yesterday and I drove by a club called 'Mundy's.' They have music and dancing every Friday and Saturday night. I don't know if we'll like it but they have dancing."

"Yeah! Maybe that's where everybody goes."

Sarah was busy helping Uncle Artie make popcorn as Bess and I left for Mundy's. Yes! We found our gold mine. The place was packed, the music loud and the dance floor jumping, exactly what we were looking for. The staff was entertainingly funny, making regular appearances on top of the bar advertising the special for the moment. They made a point to memorize our names and treated us like we've been coming for years. Mundy's captured the pure party atmosphere and became our regular Friday night destination.

One Friday night while Bess and I were dancing someone tapped her on the shoulder and she walked away and left me dancing with a stranger. I danced all night with Bess and my new dance partner. Towards the end of the evening we found a quieter place away from the speakers to visit.

As I held my safe Gin and Tonic, Ben and I introduced ourselves and performed the normal chit chat. He was also divorced and had two daughters. Kelly was eight, the same age as Sarah, and Megan was thirteen. He grew up in the Berkshires and was an engineer at General Electric in Pittsfield, Massachusetts. His sister was a teacher and taught two of Arlo Guthrie's kids. I found this tidbit the most interesting. I gave him my phone number, and the next week he called and asked me out to dinner. We went to the Candlelight Inn, located nearby in Lenox. I enjoyed his dry wit and sense of humor.

After we had a few dates under our belt we made plans to visit Balance Rock Park with the girls. It was amazing to witness the famous "Balance Rock" not falling over and the other curious boulders deposited by the glaciers of prehistoric times. It was a warm fall day in New England, and Ben and I walked ankle deep in a kaleidoscope of leaves. We watched the girls size each other up without speaking a word. Finally Kelly broke the ice and asked Sarah a question. She answered and Kelly asked another. Sarah said something funny, and the laughter started. The lines of communication opened. All three were now sharing enthusiastically the stories of their lives as they tried to climb Balance Rock.

Ben loved weekend outings with the girls and during our first year together we visited Mount Greylock a few times. At 3,500 feet, it was the highest point in Massachusetts and the best workout one would never pay for. Another popular place we liked to visit was The Mark Twain House & Museum in Hartford, Connecticut. I loved walking through the home where Samuel Clemens lived for twenty years in the late 1800s. My favorite picture of the three girls together was taken on the side lawn in front of Mark Twain's house. The girls were decked out wearing the largest smiles their faces would hold. The five of us spent our weekends together exploring the postage-stamp-sized states surrounding us and it didn't take long before the girls relationship moved from friendship to sisterhood.

I was not head over heels in love with Ben. He was more of an acquired taste. I was always weighing the pros and cons of our relationship. The pros: he was a good father, enjoyed family outings, loved to cook and he appeared to love me. The cons: my voice had little significance in our relationship. Where was my red flag? Actually, an army of red flags were parading in front of me and I chose to ignore them. After we spent our first night together I purchased a toothbrush for him to keep at my place. I thought it was a nice endearing gesture. The next day I drove home from work and into my driveway to find Ben with a truck full of his belongings.

"Ben, what are you doing?"

"I'm moving in."

"Why are you moving in? We haven't even talked about it."

"I thought you were saying to move in when you bought me a toothbrush."

"No, I was welcoming you into the next level of our relationship with a personal gift. I wasn't asking you to move in."

"How about if we discuss it tonight and whatever you decide will be fine with me."

"Okay."

That evening he began his case, we were perfect together, we have the same interests, the girls like each other and then he said, "No matter what I'm doing, I want to do it with you."

It was too soon for me but I helped him move his stuff in the next day even though I was uncomfortable with how fast our relationship was moving. He loved me. Wasn't that what I was looking for? Someone to love me?

One afternoon Ben and I were walking around Historic Lenox, when we stopped in front of a three-story mansion with an APARTMENT FOR RENT sign out front. We had talked about moving into a larger place because my apartment was too small for the five of us. We walked to the nearest phone and called the number on the sign. The owner was an attorney in Pittsfield and he agreed to meet us at the property in fifteen minutes.

We toured the apartment and fell in love with the three-story mansion converted into four apartments. Our unit was a two-story on the second and third floors. It was spacious with built-ins and trim work only found in a house built in the late 1800s. Besides hardwood floors throughout and a wood-burning fireplace in the living room, we had a formal dining room, four bedrooms, and a sunroom.

We started packing and moved within the month. Kelly and Megan spent our last night in Lee with us and joined us the next day as we moved into our mansion on Old Stockbridge Road, not far from Emily Vanderbilt's summer home. Ben sent the girls into the apartment and said, "Go pick out your rooms, and we'll be up in a few minutes."

Megan yelled, "I found my room." We followed her voice to the bedroom across from the living room on the second floor.

"Nice room Megan and you couldn't ask for a better view looking out onto our neighbor's flower garden. What kind of furniture should we be looking for?"

"I don't need much, just a bed, nightstand, and a desk with a lamp. I'm getting lots of homework this year and it'll be great to have a quiet place to work. Thanks guys for my own room."

We heard Sarah and Kelly running down the stairs and soon they were inspecting Megan's new room.

"You'll be the only one sleeping on this floor. Will that scare you?"

"No, Kelly, I don't get scared anymore. I'll be far from you guys so I won't have to hear you giggling all night long, and that suits me just fine."

"Dad, Dody, come see the room Sarah and I picked out!"

Sarah and Kelly enjoyed exploring Lenox, famous for their quaint New England shops while I put their bedroom together. Our new home sat on a large yard with our own private sledding hill. The icing on the cake was having Tanglewood in our back yard. We often heard the Boston Pops practicing or performing a concert without ever leaving home. Sometimes we walked to Tanglewood and watched them play from a blanket on their lawn. I never would have thought in a million years that someday I'd be lying in bed listening to the Boston Pops perform the "1812 Overture" complete with cannons. It was the best! In the fall Sarah started fourth grade in a new school, and a month later Ben and I married on the side yard.

22

A Bad Move

WHILE WE LIVED IN LENOX, I still worked at E. Caligari and Son in Great Barrington. My fellow bookkeepers, Denise, Brooke, and Martha, and I became the best of friends. When Ben traveled, we had pajama parties at our place. We ordered pizza, rented a couple chic flicks and sipped wine by the warmth from the fire. One day at work the discussion of facial hair came up and I said, "I've never kissed anyone with a mustache. I think it would tickle my nose and I'd start sneezing."

"Are you kidding?" Denise looked surprised.

"No, lots of women don't like men with facial hair. Why is that so hard to believe?"

"Dody, you've never kissed anyone with a mustache?"

"No."

"What about Ben?"

"What about Ben? He doesn't have a mustache."

"Yes he does."

And trying to stop laughing, Denise said, "You tell us tomorrow if he has a mustache or not."

I was surprised to see Ben wearing a mustache when he came into the house that night. After being together for two years, I didn't picture him with one.

Denise was the office manager and I covered her work load when she went on her two week vacation. We spent one day going over her check list as she showed me how to do payroll, pay bills and print out the daily reports. I remember walking into the office the day she returned and she said, "Looks like everything went well while I was gone. I couldn't find one mistake." All of the printed reports were neatly placed on her desk and I panicked inside. I thought that morning was my first day of covering her responsibilities, but it was her first day back from vacation. Where was I during the last two weeks when I wasn't here doing her work? How did it all get done? Why did I block out those two weeks? This was the first time I was aware of losing significant time in my life. I was still scared as I drove home that day, what was wrong with me? How much time was I losing? Why was I losing time? I told Ben about it that night and he tried to put my fears to rest.

"You're okay, honey. In time you'll remember the two weeks. You were probably so stressed out about getting your work and Denise's work completed each day that you didn't even stop to think about it."

I thought to myself, *Let it go, maybe I shouldn't be advertising this*. The next morning I sat in the living room watching the news and drinking my coffee. For the past ten years, this was how I liked starting my work day, relaxed and not hurried. The news just finished a story and I thought to myself, *What did they say? Oh, well, I missed it*. A new report just finished, *What did they say?* I watched the news for fifteen more minutes trying to comprehend one sentence spoken.

Over the next few weeks I tested myself and discovered I could not retain what the anchor person said each morning. I heard talking but it sounded like gibberish. It wasn't so much that I couldn't retain the information, I didn't understand what was being said. It was like watching the news on a Japanese channel instead of our local broadcast. I didn't know what to make of it. In every other area of my life I seemed okay. I enjoyed work, Sarah, weekends with the kids, and Ben. I thought I was aware of my surroundings, until Denise went on vacation the next year and I filled in again. She came back after two weeks and all her work was done correctly, and just like before, I had no memory of doing it. It felt like that strange day when I woke up on the side lawn at school. I popped up outside wearing my cheerleader uniform and Christine was showing us a new routine. I was confused and sat on the grass trying to figure out what had just happened. The last thing I remembered was sitting in science, my last class of the day and I was wearing my peach-colored slacks and a brown sweater. When did I change into my uniform? It hurt my head to try to figure it out and then Christine yelled for me to get off my butt and help make the pyramid. I also remembered that popping up from time to time was a regular occurrence in high school. It was impossible to figure out what was happening and the thought never entered my mind that I was losing time. The moment that I was aware of showing up in new place disappeared almost immediately. Quickly I lost the memory of waking up.

Sarah, Ben, and I were happy in our apartment in Lenox. Many evenings after work Ben and I visited with our neighbors sitting outside and sharing stories of the day. We were surrounded by good people and Sarah was busy with friends from school either at their homes or ours. We lived between Ben's work at General Electric in Pittsfield and my job in Great Barrington.

Some time during the year we moved to Pittsfield, Massachusetts. I have no idea why we moved from Lenox. I don't remember looking for an apartment or discussing it. I may not remember it, but it happened. Did Ben fill boxes at night and on the weekends? Did I help? It would take a minimum of five weeks to pack up the apartment in Lenox and unpack and decorate at the new place in Pittsfield. That's five weeks gone out of my life. I don't remember waking up in a new place but, I did feel drugged when we lived in Pittsfield. I was confused and disoriented most of the time and I felt Lost. Rage was returning, Happy still visited but Lost replaced Depression. It appeared my mental state was getting worse.

Sarah started fifth grade in a new school and I had no memory of it. One day towards the end of the school year she refused to leave the apartment and wouldn't tell me why. On the fourth day she planned to stay home, I stayed home with her. We sat on the sofa all morning together and I tried to get her to confide in me. Finally, after hours of my prodding she started to open up.

"Honey, you can't stay home from school forever. I know something happened, please tell me. Is someone picking on you? Did someone hurt you? Are the kids making fun of you? Whatever it is we'll fix it." Sarah started to cry.

"What is it, honey?"

"I came home from school on Monday and grabbed my small pink ball and went to the basement to wait for Elise. We like to play in the basement hall because it's wider and no one yells at us there. I was throwing the ball against the wall when a bunch of boys came into the building and pushed me into the laundry room. They turned the light out and started putting their hands all over me. I cried real hard and someone turned the light on, and they all ran out."

I held her close.

"Can you tell me what they did to you?"

"They just touched me, all of them with their hands at the same time. Nothing more than that happened because the light came on."

"Did one of the boys turn the light on, or did someone come in from the hall?"

"I don't know. I just ran as fast as I could."

"My baby, my poor baby. I'm so sorry. I'm sorry, honey. Do you know who any of the boys were?

"Yeah, Jake was one of them."

"Do you know Jake?"

"Not really. He goes to my school and he's always in our parking lot on his skateboard."

"The one that wears a black leather jacket?"

"Yea, him."

I remembered Jake. He dressed in black jeans, black t-shirt, and a black leather jacket. His hair was dark, straight and slicked back. He looked like a little hood from the fifties, and I would guess him to be near Sarah's age. I often saw him hanging out in the parking lot on his skateboard or walking around our building. I wondered why he always looked at the ground. I felt sorry for him. Now, I was angry and wanted to find him.

"Sarah, we need to call the police."

"No." she screamed. "They'll hurt me again and you'll make it worse if you do that."

"Sarah, we have to do something. We need to at least talk to his parents. Those boys hurt you. They forced you into a room and they scared you. We have to report this."

"No. That won't help. Mostly they just scared me. If you love me you won't tell anyone."

I didn't know what to do. Maybe they would hurt her again if I went to the police or to Jake's parents. I talked with Ben that evening and he wanted to talk to Jake's parents. The next day was Saturday. Ben, Sarah, and I all went outside and Jake was in the parking lot. As soon as he saw us he started walking away. We let him create some distance between us and then we followed in his direction. As we walked farther from our apartment building the neighborhood took on a new ambiance. Houses held less paint, a mattress leaned against the side of a house covering up a window and we passed a bar on the corner. *Was it as dirty inside as it was on the outside?* The windows were boarded up, but they were open for business. Dead plants in broken pots sat near a front door. *A lifetime ago she attempted to make her home look pretty.* I felt sorry for the cats that looked out windows at us.

We watched Jake walk up a driveway and towards the back of a house. Ben knocked on the front door. A blanket hung in front of the picture window. The front yard was dirt like its neighbors', void of green grass. Not even the weeds survived here. Ben knocked again. A man looking as run down as his home opened the door.

"Hello, sir. Are you Jake's father?"

"Yeah, who's asking?"

"I'm Ben Jordon, and your son and four other boys forced my step-daughter into the laundry room of our apartment building. She is now afraid to leave the apartment."

"Sounds like you have a problem."

"Your son carries some responsibility in this matter."

"That's not how I see it," and he slammed the door in Ben's face.

That's as much as we did. Sarah was adamant about not saying anything more to anybody else. Why didn't I find help for her, especially then?

I drove Sarah to school everyday and picked her up every afternoon. Two weeks after Sarah told us about the boys in the laundry room Ben accepted a position at Hamilton Standard in Connecticut. I thought the timing was perfect; Sarah won't have to worry about those boys anymore.

Just before we moved to Connecticut, I overheard Ben talking on the phone with a co-worker about a roast GE was having in his honor.

"Ben, that's great. GE is giving you a roast. I can't wait. When is it?"

"It's going to be stupid. You don't want to go. It's just a little office farewell party."

114

"So? I'm your wife, I can go to your farewell party. A roast will be fun."

I thought he was just being humble saying he didn't want me to go. I didn't know he meant he didn't want me to go until I went. The afternoon of his roast I walked into the banquet room and found a place to sit. It started out an entertaining afternoon with funny gag gifts and inside jokes I didn't understand. Ben, being an engineer, one of his coworkers told the joke, "Ben came to work constipated one day and being the good engineer that he was, worked it out with a slide rule." *Gross*.

Next, his boss stood behind the podium and spoke. "Ben, you will be missed greatly by your peers and because of your work here in Quality Control, overseeing the building of aircraft engines, your fellow workers have all chipped in for two round-trip tickets to Disneyland on Amtrak."

After the roast a reception line was formed to say goodbye to Ben. I stood next to him and was not prepared for what was about to happen. After shaking Ben's hand a co-worker asked, "And who are you?"

"I'm Dody, Ben's wife."

"What? Ben has a wife? When did that happen?"

"Over a year ago."

I repeated this conversation with Ben's peers for the next thirty minutes.

I didn't know how to absorb this new information. *My husband didn't tell anyone at work he was married, not even Mel, who shared an office with him.* I was embarrassed standing in front of all those people out in the open and not being Ben's little secret anymore.

That evening at home, I screamed and kicked the wall, the furniture, and Ben.

"How come you never told anyone you were married? Didn't it ever come up in conversation?"

"I keep my private life separate from my work."

"Why?"

"Nobody needs to know my business."

"Ben are you lying to me?"

"No, I never lie. I don't believe in lying. Sometimes I don't give all the information, but I never lie."

"What information are you withholding now?"

"None."

I beat on Ben with a vengeance screaming, "How come I'm a secret?" *My husband didn't care about me anymore than my parents had.* "I hate you."

As I pounded on him, he stood there taking every punch. He didn't try to stop me or defend himself. He just stood there looking sheepish and smiled.

After the roast I never did much with Ben when it involved his work and I didn't push for it either. I'd learned my lesson well. I never enjoyed accompanying him to a business function where he was expected to bring his wife. He rarely sat at the table with me and when he did his back was always towards me while he looked elsewhere.

23

Dog Poop

DURING THE SUMMER WE FOUND an apartment in Enfield, Connecticut, close to Ben's new employer and even closer to his daughters, Megan and Kelly. I accepted a position at First Brands in East Hartford. Our girls saw each other more often and sometimes Sarah spent the night at their home. It was rare if the three of them didn't spend the weekend together and now that we lived closer, we saw Kelly and Megan in the middle of the week.

In the fall Sarah started the sixth grade in a new school. It was a struggle every morning trying to get her to go. She hated waiting for the bus with the other kids and one morning she informed us, "I'm not going to school anymore."

"Why not?" I asked.

"The kids are mean to me at the bus stop. At first they laughed at me and made fun of my clothes and backpack, and yesterday, Tim picked up dog poop and threw it at me. Mom, they're throwing dog poop at me. I can't go and I won't."

Ben said, "Grab your backpack. We're going to the bus stop. Nobody throws dog poop at you and gets away with it."

Sarah pointed out Tim, and Ben went over to confront him. He asked for his phone number and Tim gave it. That evening Ben called Tim's parents and the three of us walked over to his house.

"Mom, do we have to go. Isn't it enough that Ben talked to Tim this morning? I don't think he's going to be mean to me anymore. Can't we just drop it?"

Ben said, "No, we're going and that's it."

Shawn and Tammy answered the door after I rang the bell. They were friendly and a little cautious as they led us to the dining room. After we sat down, Ben began, "There was an incident at the bus stop yesterday. It involved somebody throwing dog poop and it landing on Sarah."

"I'm sorry that happened to you Sarah. Who threw the dog poop?" Shawn asked.

Sarah didn't say anything and Ben said, "Tim, do you know who threw the dog poop?"

"Yeah. I did."

"Tim, you apologize right now to Sarah." Both his parents scolded.

"Sarah, I'm sorry."

"That's okay."

After we discussed the dog poop throwing, and Tim apologized to Sarah, they ran off to his room and left us adults to get to know each other better. After two hours Tammy ordered pizza and the four of us laughed and talked all evening. Ben looked at his watch and said, "Can you believe its eleven o'clock?"

While we were walking home that night, Sarah said, "Tim and I are best friends now."

"Wow! That's amazing. I'm so glad. Well this worked out nice. We all found new friends today."

"You know what Tim told me tonight?"

"What."

"He said he threw the dog poop at me because he liked me and he was just trying to be funny. He didn't mean to hit me."

"Boys are strange creatures aren't they?" Ben interjected.

Having Tim for a friend helped Sarah meet other kids and she started to enjoy school again. She even acquired a new best friend, Jan. Sarah now had a full social life. She was either riding her bike or on long walks with Jan or swimming at the pool with Tim. Her favorite activity was roller skating. She loved school and looked forward to going everyday. I remember Halloween that year. Sarah and Jan went trick-or-treating and came back with their pillow cases full. I hadn't seen Sarah laugh so hard or be that happy since she was with Jason and the boys. It was great to see her excited.

We loved living in Enfield, so Ben and I started looking for a house to buy. We were disappointed to find out we couldn't afford one. Ben traveled to Minnesota almost every week for business so I made plans to go with him on his next trip. My father and his wife, Peg, lived in Burnsville, a suburb of Minneapolis. I hadn't seen them for ten years, but we kept in touch by talking on the phone every so often. Planning a trip to see my father and Peg gave me something else to think about besides the house we couldn't afford in Enfield. Dad stopped climbing the corporate ladder and was an architect again working with a number of builders in the area. As we flew closer to Minnesota, I was drawn to the land. By the time the plane touched the ground I was overwhelmed by a magnetic pull at my body. When I walked off the plane I knew I was home. The people were friendly, the lifestyle slower and so many lakes. We discovered not only could we afford to buy a house, we could build one. Ben requested a transfer to Minnesota, showing on paper how cost effective it was for Hamilton Standard to have him located here. His request was approved and we started making plans to move to Minnesota after we found a half acre on a lake three miles from Dad and Peg's place. Dad started drawing house plans for us.

Sarah cried every day and tried to talk us out of moving. A day didn't go by that she didn't try to change our minds. She tried right up until the day we flew out of Hartford. Her words fell on deaf ears. Why didn't I listen to her? Was I out of my mind? Why was I doing this to her again, especially now when she was the happiest she'd ever been? Why couldn't I stop moving? But we didn't change our plans and Sarah was overwhelmed with sadness and anger. This was the move she would not bounce back from.

24

Too Little, Too Late

WE MOVED TO MINNESOTA IN JULY of 1988, Sarah was almost twelve. She stayed in her bedroom for the rest of the summer and on many days she never left her bed.

In the fall Sarah started seventh grade in a new school and her depression worsened. I wouldn't learn until years later that she was being bullied everyday. She didn't attend school much that year and never went a full week. I met with her school counselor a few times, but no one had any ideas how to help Sarah. She was angry. I rarely saw her and she seldom talked to me. By now she had learned not to trust me to make good decisions when it concerned her life and she desperately wanted to live with her dad. I called Jesse after the school year ended, and he agreed to have Sarah move in with him and his wife in Upstate, New York. Once Sarah learned she was going to live with her father, her spirits improved. She put so much hope into moving in with her dad that she anticipated her life getting better. What did every child want? To feel loved and cared for, secure, protected, safe. To have a voice or at least to be considered when decisions that affect the whole family are made. I wasn't able to give Sarah any of that, and now she was hoping to receive from her father the love and attention she was literally starving for.

In the fall Sarah started eighth grade in a new school. She lived with her dad for one year and then asked if she could move back to Minnesota. The move to New York didn't improve her life, it only added more heartache to it.

At the same time, Sarah was returning from Upstate New York, Kelly and Megan asked to move in with us. That summer the five of us were together again, but we were not the family in Minnesota that we were in Connecticut.

Ben's girls brought with them the anger they felt towards us for moving and leaving them. They were angry at Sarah because she had moved with us and was able to live with their dad while they couldn't. We lived together for almost a year with the silence sometimes louder than the girls fighting. Sarah, Kelly, and Megan were all suffering from deep wounds, and we knew they were hanging on by a thread. Ben and I decided to separate and make helping the girls our priority. Kelly and Megan stayed in the house with Ben and I found an apartment in Burnsville for Sarah and me.

Our surroundings improved after we moved out but my relationship with Sarah did not. She was gone most of the time and when she was home it was behind closed doors in her bedroom. I kept telling myself, *she's a teenager and teenagers don't like their parents. Her behavior is normal. In time she'll like me again.*

Ben received a letter saying we were going to lose our Homestead status because we had two residences. This would greatly increase our property tax, so we made the decision to divorce and remarry when the girls were all in a good place.

In the fall Sarah started ninth grade in a new school. For the next couple years she tried a few more schools and didn't like any of them. When she turned sixteen, she quit and found a full-time job. After a few years she received her GED.

Sarah and I moved to St. Paul after a year to be closer to our work. I was the office manager at a mental health clinic and Sarah worked the front desk at a downtown hotel. We loved St.

Paul. It was a big city that felt like a small town. A year later I bought a condo in a Victorian house in the Irving Park neighborhood and Sarah moved into her first apartment one block away. She lived on the sixth floor and we waved to each other from our living room windows when we talked on the phone at night. Restaurants and shops were within walking distance and we often met for dinner after work. Our favorite activity was visiting the Science Museum together.

At this time in my life Happy hung around a lot. Rage, Depression, and Lost seldom appeared. My head hurt less and I didn't feel confused. My job was rewarding and I felt all grown up owning my own home. I remodeled the bathroom, installed a new wood floor in the kitchen and gave every room a fresh coat of paint. This was the first time I lived alone and I liked making all the decisions. I read a lot and had a nice social life going to the movies with friends or shopping. During the five years that Ben and I were divorced, we saw each other a couple times a month. He traveled Monday through Friday for work so that gave me time to carve out a life that I wanted to have filled with my interest.

After Sarah and I moved out of the house, Megan stayed for another year and then moved back to Connecticut and enrolled at Southern Connecticut University where she later graduated. Kelly dropped out of school and moved back home with her mom in Connecticut and received her GED.

It appeared that our girls were all in a good place.

25

The Sailor

FIVE YEARS AFTER OUR DIVORCE, Ben and I remarried. We had the ceremony at the condo, and my father, Sarah, Megan, Kelly, and our closest friends attended our wedding.

Ben moved in and we sold the house in Burnsville. His employer Hamilton Standard went through a major downsizing and that added to Ben's work load considerably. We were both worried about his health. He looked tired and lost valuable weight.

We talked about what to do to lessen the stress in his life and after many discussions we agreed on purchasing a sailboat. We rented a slip on Lake Pepin in Pepin, Wisconsin, a ninety-minute drive from St. Paul. Lake Pepin is the largest lake on the entire Mississippi River smack in the middle of Minnesota and Wisconsin surrounded by bluffs.

We wanted a place to go to every weekend for play and relaxation. I loved being on the water, and Ben looked twenty years younger again. We learned that stress was allergic to boats and water, so both Ben and I welcomed our new lifestyle. We turned vacation days into many long weekends on the lake sailing and swimming during the day and dinner with friends at night. Sometimes we'd go out to the middle of the lake with three other sailboats and one would let down their anchor. We lined up in a row and tied our boats together. The first boat on the end served cocktails and hors d'oeuvres. The second boat provided the salad and breads. The third one grilled the main course, and dessert was served on the fourth boat.

The continuous rocking in the water created the most tranquil, calming sleep. When we knew a storm was near we loosened all the lines tied to the cleats on the dock to achieve maximum wave action.

Life was good. Ben still traveled every week but now he had something to look forward to every weekend. After a year of sailing, I started my own graphic art business "Sailing Concepts" and worked out of the condo. I received pictures and logos in the mail from sailors around the world. After I reworked their photos I applied them to polo shirts, t-shirts, jackets, canvas bags, mouse pads, or coffee mugs. I advertised my business in the international *Sailing* magazine. Sailing Concepts did well and provided me the creative outlet I needed.

Peg, my father's wife, died of cancer a year after we moved to Minnesota and eventually Dad moved to St. Paul to live closer to us. Every Tuesday evening I picked Sarah up and we drove over to get Grandpa. We stopped at a few places while Dad ran his errands for the week and then we arrived at Dunham's in West St. Paul for their famous tacos. After dinner, it was off to the pool room and Sarah took care of the evening's music via the jukebox. I couldn't believe we actually had a routine where I spent an evening every week with my daughter and father. We shot pool and enjoyed jokes and laughter with the other patrons at Dunham's. Sarah spent a few weekends on the boat with us and for a week one summer my sister Kathy and her family came from New York for a Lake Pepin vacation. Dad loved the sailboat and every so often he and his friend came aboard for cards in the afternoon.

For three and a half years this was my life and it was feeling pretty darn wonderful. I was in a good place.

During the five years that Ben and I were divorced and while I was the office manager at a mental health clinic in St. Paul, I asked Sawyer, my favorite of all the therapists, if he would hypnotize me to help me stop smoking. I knew he did this for some of his clients. He had to refuse because we worked together and as he put it, "You never know what might surface when you're under hypnosis." He recommended Hannah to me. I made an appointment with Hannah and after a few sessions, she asked me if I would like to work on anything else.

"Yes, I want to stop moving. I want to stop changing homes, jobs, states, and husbands. I don't seem to be able to stop."

I worked with Hannah on many issues: my mother, my father, my fear of success, Sarah, my past husbands, my low self-esteem, my sadness. The list continued to grow and I saw Hannah once a week for three and a half years until we had everything covered and I was a much stronger person.

26

The First Repressed Memory

I STOOD FROZEN IN MY DINING ROOM as I listened to the words spoken, "You dirty little girl. You've been a bad girl. You disgust me. You naughty little girl. I'm going to have to punish you." It was a Friday afternoon and I was hearing someone talking to a little girl and I didn't like what I heard. I went to all the windows in my second-story condo trying to find the person saying these words to probably a very scared little child. It was early November and chilly outside. I opened each window, but I couldn't find the person saying these awful things. No one was outside and after a while I had to accept the fact that this voice was coming from inside my head and these words had been said to me when I was little.

I sat in the dining room until Ben came home that evening. He walked in and came over for his welcome-home kiss, "What's wrong?" I told him the words I heard that afternoon and he said, "It sounds like something someone would say while hurting a child."

"That's what I thought, and I think they were said to me." It was very unnerving to say the least. "Now what do we do?"

"Let's wait and see if anything else happens," he suggested.

We watched the ten o'clock news that night and started getting ready for bed. After I went through the house making sure all outside doors were locked, pilots still lit on the stove and lights out, I jumped into bed. Ben leaned over to kiss me goodnight and I smacked him hard across the face. For a second, it wasn't Ben in bed with me. I felt terrible for hitting him but we both knew this was the beginning of something.

The next morning I woke up and I wasn't myself, nothing felt the same. I didn't know that my world had changed that morning, and I walked out of one life and entered another. A new past and present were emerging. I called Hannah and told her what had transpired and she said she would call me back. After some research, she called the next day and told me about a woman's group that focused on childhood sexual abuse and gave me June's number. I phoned June and learned about the women's group. She and another therapist facilitated the group once a week. They allowed for no more than six women at a time, and a spot was going to open up the first week in February if I could wait that long. This group was highly recommended so I decided to wait. I met with June right away to do the intake and to start my individual therapy sessions with her. My life was in shutdown mode and I couldn't wait to get unstuck.

After I hung up with June, I called my dad to invite him out to lunch. I drove over to his place and we walked the skyway system from his apartment building into Dayton's Restaurant. After lunch I told him memories of childhood sexual abuse had surfaced and I was starting therapy to work through it. He instantly got ill, lost his balance and fell onto a bench near by. "Do you know who it is?"

"No, not yet, but my gut tells me it's either you, Artie, or Mr. Stewart."

"I hope it's not me. I don't feel well and need to go home."

"Dad, if it's you, we can deal with it and work through it. I love you and that won't change."

A few weeks after the memories first surfaced, Artie called me to say he had bone cancer. The doctors were very optimistic because he had four siblings. Surely one of us would be a bone marrow match. I didn't tell him about the repressed memories. I was still trying to make sense of my life and now he was fighting for his. He called after we were all tested to say no one was a match, but it was one-hundred percent clear we all came from the same mother and father. This was always a joke with us because none of us looked like our parents or each other.

The next summer Sarah, Ben, and I flew to Massachusetts to see Artie, Bess, and Evan. Artie was bald from the treatments and it was good to be with my big brother again. I would not entertain the thought for a second that he might die. I knew he wouldn't. I still hadn't told him about the sexual abuse. He had so much on his plate and I didn't want to add more. *We'll talk about it later.*

One of my new memories that surfaced was standing next to Artie's bed crying. He would say, "Come on up here" and hold me until I stopped crying. Once I stopped crying he would tell me jokes until I couldn't stop laughing. Once I was laughing, he told me how wonderful life will be when we were old enough to leave this house. We talked a lot about our dreams of a better place. "Our life will be just the way we want it," I can still hear him saying.

"When I'm grown up I'm going to have a cupboard in my kitchen filled with nothing but candy. I'm going to have children who have happy lives filled with lots of love and hugs." Artie and I lived this life of me showing up at his bed crying for years.

Next, I remembered the times before I went into Artie's room, seeing my dad leave my bedroom and walking down the stairs. I went into Artie's room as soon as I heard Dad snoring and then I remembered how much my body hurt. It hurt to walk. The day after Dad's visits I soaked in the tub hoping that the water would take away the pain.

Ben, Sarah, and I made plans to spend Christmas with Artie, Bess, and Evan. I couldn't wait to see him again. He called in November to congratulate us on our newly elected Governor Jessie Ventura. "Minnesota must be a wonderful place to live to have such open minded people to elect someone like Jessie."

"Minnesota is wonderful, I wish you all lived here. I can't wait to see you next month. I love you."

"I love you too."

Bess called me five days before Christmas. Artie had died.

27

Artie

A FTER ARTIE DIED THE MEMORIES CAME flooding in. I had just lost my savoir and was beginning to understanding that I survived growing up in our house because of Artie. He rarely left me at home when he went out. I was the only girl allowed in the "Boys Only Club." I grew up climbing trees and playing army at Roosevelt Field on the tanks and hiding behind sand bags so not to get shot. We walked to the candy store close by or rode our bikes to the one farther away. I rode alongside him while he did his paper route and we caught snakes in the fields to put in our aquarium in the garage.

When Artie started dating, he brought me on most of his dates. The girl's parents especially liked this. What a fine young man to bring his little sister on dates with him. Artie showed up at a girl's home to have her parents answer the door with suspicion on their faces only to be replaced with, "So happy to meet you!" after he introduced me. Artie took his date and me to the movies, Coney Island, and my favorite place, the beach. He even got permission to take me to work with him when he landed a job at a nearby country club. I was allowed to bring my best friend, Deborah, and we sat by the pool and talked and swam all day long. Artie stopped by now and then to say hi and to see if we needed anything.

I had no idea how much he took care of me during those years growing up. I realize now, Artie and I saved each other by bonding and talking. We spent as much time as we could outside the house and we talked. We talked when our parents went out and we talked when they fell asleep. Kathy didn't have anyone in the family to talk to. It must have been very hard for her growing up trying to have friends and taking care of two little boys. Bill and Bob may have leaned on each other when they were young. Our parents taught us not to complain or feel sad and to always appreciate what we had. We were punished if caught saying negative things about them. It was safest not to talk at all.

After Sarah and I moved to Massachusetts, one morning at dawn, Artie and I went fishing. We were in a light misty fog trolling in the boat near shore when Artie said to me, "Remember when dad use to beat me at the bottom of the stairs in Garden City?"

"Yea, I hated that. I wanted to kill him."

"It was okay, I was more focused on not crying instead of feeling the pain. He was a stupid drunk man beating a kid and I wasn't going to give him the satisfaction of breaking down. I was going to beat him by not crying. I also have to credit him for my success. I grew up wanting to prove him wrong that I wasn't a bum. Who knows, if he hadn't been the jerk he was, maybe I wouldn't have been successful."

Then Artie shared another story with me.

"Bess is amazing. Sometimes I'm out of control and I'm a real bastard. I scream at her, cutting her down with piercing words. Once my rage comes out, I can't stop it until I've completely destroyed something and most often, it's my wife."

"I know what you mean, I think we all have a little of Mom in us and it comes out from time to time."

"Remember when Bess and I visited Mom a few years ago? It was the first time she met our mother and of course there was a scene. Mom got angry about something and kicked us out. After that trip, whenever my rage and anger surfaced, all Bess had to say was, "Art, you're pulling a Marilyn," and I snapped out of my emotional spiral."

Later that day, Artie shared his crying tape with me. As an adult he still had many collections, but now he was also a connoisseur of wine, movies, and music. "This is my crying tape."

"What's that?"

"It's filled with songs that make me cry. You know that feeling when you're on the verge of crying, but it won't happen. And, you know all you need is a good hard cry, but it won't come. When I feel like that, I listen to my crying tape and the tears come flooding out. I feel this great release and then I can go on with my day." He made me a copy of his crying tape.

Artie's funeral was the first week in January. Ben, Sarah, Kelly, and I went to it. I was angry that neither of my parents went. I never heard of parents not attending the funeral of their child.

The day of Artie's funeral was the most painful day of my life. I needed to tell him thank you. I wanted to hug him and say, "You saved me. Because of you, I learned what love was. I knew protection because of you. I didn't disappear forever because of you. I learned to dream and hang on for a better place. You were all I had and it was a lot."

28

Good-Bye Mom and Dad

EBRUARY FINALLY CAME AND WITH MIXED FEELINGS I went to my first women's group meeting. I still didn't like to talk in public. Would they kick me out if I didn't talk? Needless to say, I was a nervous wreck. We took turns going around our little circle introducing ourselves. I was in very good company which was even more intimidating. One woman was an English professor and playwright, another owned her own restaurant in the Uptown area of Minneapolis, and another was an executive at Honeywell. The Fourth woman worked for the family nursery business, and the fifth one was an attorney. I listened to these woman take turns talking about things I understood. I was struggling with the same issues they had and for the first time I understood why life was so hard for me and it had nothing to do with being crazy.

That evening after my first meeting I sat in our living room curled up at the end of the sofa and wrote this letter to my parents. My life had shutdown, I barely functioned and trust and sexual desires disappeared. I had no idea I was holding these thoughts so close to the surface as the words poured out of me onto paper.

Dear Mom & Dad,
This letter is for the two of you who brought me into your world, and by law I had to live with you. It's now time to let go

of you both. You hurt me very much. I was raped of my virginity when I was little. I was raped of self-esteem, self-worth, security, safeness, and love. I was raped of accomplishments and a job well done. I was raped of all the goodness I started out with and stripped of who I was. You took a little child who was born to you and took turns destroying an innocent, trusting, vulnerable little girl.

The world you presented to me was one filled with fear, pain, and sadness. You taught me to fail, and you told me I was unworthy. I learned not to trust and not to feel. I learned to take care of you. I have a lot to unlearn and I have a lot to learn about me and the world I live in. I will learn to allow good into my life and how to have healthy relationships. I will learn how to have sex with my husband and how to trust myself and my husband.

I look at my body in the mirror and I see the ugliest body ever to exist. There is no body uglier than mine. I was taught by you, Dad, that my body has to be perfect. I was taught by you that the only thing I had to offer the world was a perfect, beautiful body. I tried all my life to have this perfect body, only it kept getting uglier and uglier. I'm letting go of you both and your sick world. I'm letting go of the "little shit" you referred to me when I lived in your house. I'm letting go of your words and your touches on my body. I spent most of my life trying not to be a disappointment to you and trying to get you to like me and be proud of me.

I will not let you have the role of parent in my life. I am going back to see that little girl who was born on August 10, 1953. She came into the world to experience good, and good she is going to have. I was not created to offer the world a vagina to be played with and used and abused. I am not a body with a hole for other people to stick things into. I am a whole body, a whole person. I will parent me now. I tell myself it is sad that I lived the life I did, and it is now time to let go of what molded me and let the woman evolve. My voice will be the strongest voice I hear. I will love and cherish the person I am. I will take care of myself and do good to me.

I will think about the hurt and pain I feel and decide where it is coming from. When I hear Dad's and Mom's voices, I will not give it power. When I don't allow good things in, I will STOP, see where that is coming from and say, "You are wrong Dad and Mom. I can allow and I do allow this good into my life." I am worthy to receive love and to give love. You lied to me for too many years.

You said I am ugly . . . I say I am beautiful.

You said don't look like that . . . I say this is how I look.

You said I can't have that . . . I say I can.

You said I can't receive that gift . . . I say I will receive it.

You said I have to go with you . . . I say I don't have to go anywhere with you.

You said I am a disappointment . . . I say I can't bother with you anymore, I have much to explore.

You said I scare you . . . I say I don't scare anyone.

You said be quiet . . . I say I will talk.

You said be a good girl . . . . . .I say I am a good girl.

You said I don't deserve good things . . . I say I deserve good things, I have good things, and I will continue to receive good things.

You said therapist are quacks . . . I say only the strong will ask for help.

You said I was a slut . . . I say I was trying to find love.

You said there is NEED and there is WANT, and we should have what we need and not what we want . . . I say I have what I need and I will continue to go after my wants. I want to hear my positive voice and not your negative ones.

You told me I was selfish because I cried when you wouldn't let me receive a gift. You took away what gifts I was given. I am a gift to myself, to my husband, to my daughter, to people who meet me and to people whose lives I have touched.

You are right about one thing . . . I am a BIG disappointment to you! I failed at staying under your control. I failed at letting you have power over me. Your voice means nothing to me. I see two selfish people. I see two sad people. I see two failures.

I am starting to experience a new life. I have a husband, a daughter, two step-daughters, and three siblings very much in my life, and I am beginning to build strong, close healthy relationships with all of them. The way I see it is, I have three very strong voices inside my head, Mom's, Dad's, and my own. Dad and Mom, you don't make sense, you lie, you don't know the truth. You know bad, you know empty, you know failure. All the answers are in my voice. All the dreams and accomplishments are in my voice. What saved me in the past and what saves me now is listening to my own voice. My voice says I am good. I am beautiful. I am talented and smart. I am strong. I am sexual. I am a success because I am ME!

It is time to say good-bye to the Dad and Mom I knew, and the Dad and Mom I hoped you would be. It is time to say hello to Dad and Mom who are in my life today, but not as before. Today you are powerless over me. Today you do not influence me. Today you exist. I will not hate you. And some day I may love you again. I do not feel sorry for you. You are Dad and Mom, and I had nothing to do with that. I will allow you to be in my life. I will not allow you to hurt me in any way any more.

Yesterday's voices are gone. Tomorrow looks brighter because I listen to my voice today. I will take one day at a time, one breath at a time to walk into a day I deserve to have. I will patiently and calmly with courage evolve. I will not put demands on myself but will work toward my goals. My first goal is snuggling with my husband. He will hold me, and it is my husband holding me and not anyone else. I will hold my husband and not anyone else.

I was a wounded child crying out, FIX ME! Now I understand I am the only one who can give me the life I want. My expectations have changed. I expect my friends to live their lives and I will live mine and our paths will cross over many times . . . but what I share with my husband is special. He is not using me to fulfill his sexual pervertedness. He is my husband with sexual desires and he desires me, all of me. He wants the same thing I want, only he's already there and I'm on my way.

Good-bye Mom and Dad

After I wrote this letter to my parents with no intention of mailing it, I found it encouraging. I read this letter of affirmation every day for six months. After six months I started drawing pictures to go with the words. I ended up with a picture book of my new life. It was the beginning of finding my voice.

29

The Past Comes Forward

I WAS STILL IN SHUTDOWN MODE and was told it was natural to shut down after repressed childhood memories surfaced. I was in shock. All the ways I learned to survive and keep my insanity a secret were now irrelevant. I wasn't insane. Shutdown mode is similar to grieving the loss of a close loved one, a child or a significant other that dies without warning. I woke up and my childhood was not as I remembered it. First, I grieved the loss of my past as I knew it, and then I grieved the past that replaced it. The one filled with violence, torture, and sexual abuse. Next, came the mourning for the endings of past marriages and men that I loved. I had to mourn the loss of my childhood and my young adult years. I had to grieve the loss of my innocence as a young child and the abrupt awareness that my parents would never love me.

During my shutdown period, I didn't want to see anyone. Home was my safest place. I didn't know how to function out in the world and I didn't want to talk. How did I explain to my friends what had just happened when I was still learning what had just happened. Friends, work, and Ben were put aside while I began the healing process. The only people I let into my world were the women from my support group and my therapist. I was in the process of learning who I was and what I was made of. I wondered if I was going to sink or make it? It took all the energy I had to work towards making it.

My trust level was at zero and I was learning how to trust the world I lived in and most important how to trust myself. Group therapy is highly recommended when someone is working through childhood sexual abuse issues because trust has a chance to grow in that setting. I learned to feel safe with the women in my group and eventually we connected. The average shutdown lasts from six months to a year, mine lasted six months.

Ben had taken an early retirement and severance package from Hamilton Standard a year prior to my first repressed memory surfacing. About the time my shutdown was ending he accepted a position in North Mankato, Minnesota. We sold the condo and purchased a home on Lake Jefferson in Cleveland, Minnesota, in May of 1999. Just before we moved to Cleveland my father called to ask if I remembered who abused me. "Yes, it was you, Dad, and we can work through this. All I need is for you to say you're sorry and we'll be fine."

"You ungrateful daughter for bringing this up now," and he hung up on me. That was the last time I talked to my dad.

We moved into our new home on a spectacular lake with an assortment of wildlife we had only seen in books. We canoed around the lake and sometimes over to a restaurant near the waters edge for dinner. At times we relaxed peacefully drifting on the water in our large six-man raft. I liked taking the row boat out and being alone with my thoughts. We moved a great distance farther from Pepin, Wisconsin, where our sailboat was so we decided to sell the boat and play on the lake in our backyard. We stopped at a gas station the morning we left for Pepin to bring the sailboat home. Pizza Hut was attached to this station and Ben said, "Why don't you grab us something to eat while I fuel up." I went inside to the little convenient store and saw two isles leading to the Pizza Hut counter to my right. I went to the far isle and started to walk toward the counter to place my order. I froze at the entrance and was powerless to walk down between the round dining tables placed on the right and the booths on the left. I started to hyperventilate and was unable to breathe when Ben walked in and saw I was in trouble. He ran over and put his arms around me, "What's happening?"

After I started to relax I said, "I don't know. I couldn't move. I was terrified and I don't know why." He took my hand and we walked down the isle and placed our order. After we paid and gathered our food, we turned to walk back down the aisle and I passed an old woman sitting in the last booth. I looked at her and paused. Her mouth wasn't moving but I heard her say, "It will be okay, honey. It will be okay."

Ben and I drove away from the gas station and immediately a memory surfaced. I remembered my father finished remodeling the basement in our St. Louis home. I was five years old when he invited a group of men over and I was the entertainment. I saw myself as a little girl parading from one end of the bar to the other naked. Dad had stools at the bar and round tables set up. Men were saying how pretty I was and laughing and cheering. I remember lying down in sleeping bags with different men and feeling scared. I disappeared as the sleeping bag closed in on me.

Seeing the round tables at the gas station Pizza Hut with men sitting around them laughing and talking and me starting to walk down the aisle which must have resembled the bar top runway, brought to life this repressed memory from when I was five.

I called my mother and sister the next day and told them about that memory. They both remembered when Dad had men over to the bar in the basement. Mom said, "Sometimes they stayed for days and I had to cook for them, but I wasn't allowed in there. You were the only one allowed in the basement. The door was always locked.

In therapy I was told if I did the hard work to heal, my life could be of better quality than that of someone who had never been abused. That became my goal. I wanted to do the hard work and end up with a quality life.

Soon after Ben and I moved to Cleveland, Minnesota, our relationship took a turn for the worse. My life at home with him was mirroring his behavior towards me as if we were at a business function. He fixed his own meals, sat in the living room each evening with a magazine, concentrating deeply on what he was reading and not acknowledging my presence. Our marriage endured significant stress during the last year with my repressed memories surfacing and Ben not knowing what to do. I made an appointment for us with a marriage counselor who suggested that Ben read a few books written for the spouse of a survivor of childhood sexual abuse or he could attend a support group in the area for the spouse of a survivor. He did nothing and after a few more months of not talking to me, I asked if he wanted to stay married. He said, "Yes."

"Then I have an ultimatum for you. Sometime in the next twelve months I need you to do a positive action for our marriage (I was in no hurry). I don't care what it is. You can read a book, join a support group or sign us up for marriage counseling. Just do one thing that says you care about us." I lived the next ten months with his silence and told him when there were two months left. After being together for seventeen years, on the anniversary of my ultimatum I filed for divorce.

I did not want our marriage to end and when I was alone in the house I screamed as loud as I could, frightening our poor cats, and sobbing looking out the picture window at our beautiful lake. I didn't want to leave Ben, my home or my lake. This was new pain and I allowed myself to feel all of it, I was still focused on healing. As painful as it was to end this marriage, I knew I was doing the right thing. I would much rather live a full life alone then live with someone who pretended I didn't exist. My life was changing fast and I was finding me not hidden behind anything.

Ben accepted a new job in Pennsylvania to be closer to his girls and grandkids. He came to St. Paul to say goodbye. We talked and ended the visit with a hearty hug. We had been through a lifetime together. Just before he drove off, he rolled down his window and said, "Who knows, maybe we'll get married again in five years."

30

Shutdown and Black Holes

M Y REPRESSED MEMORIES FIRST SURFACED when I was forty-five. For the next three years hidden memories came at a steady pace into my mind. My life was unfolding before my eyes, complete with pictures, heartache, despair, and tremendous loss.

I moved into an apartment in St. Paul on Summit Avenue after I filed for divorce. I lived on the third floor of a Victorian building with beautiful views outside my large windows of the Cathedral looking majestic and the Capitol looking stately. It was a good place for me to be. I was still seeing June, my therapist and attending my woman's group once a week. I started taking writing classes at the Loft in Minneapolis and working part time at a private school in St. Paul.

My repressed memories surfaced without effort sometimes and other times not until I went through my black hole. This is my black hole. First I felt a wave of sadness pass through me and after I closed my eyes I saw myself spiraling down into a black hole. All the while pictures unfolded in my mind from my past. I allowed the tears to accompany the pain and fear I felt as a child.

I saw myself lying in my bed as a little girl and seeing my father walking out of my bedroom and turning to go down the stairs. As soon as I heard him snoring I went to Artie's room and started crying. Artie comforted me. I remembered this at forty-five.

The memory of my parents fight in Los Angeles when I was sixteen and my father screaming for my mother to unlock the door while he was pounding on it with a meat cleaver surfaced when I was forty-five.

The memory of my parent's last fight in Cattaraugus when my father tried to burn my mother to death surfaced when I was forty-seven.

After third grade I disappeared for three consecutive years, a three-year fugue. I woke up at the end of sixth grade. The memory of waking up that day in the sixth grade surfaced when I was forty-seven.

In August of 2009, I went to a retreat center to work on this book for a week. My first morning there, I sat at the desk and before I started to write, I heard the words inside my head again, "You, dirty little girl. I'm going to have to punish you." Those words first surfaced when I was forty-five, but I never knew who said them until that morning at the retreat center. I remembered my mother saying that to me as she locked me in the unfinished storage area over the garage. I heard her lock the door with me sitting on rafters in a dark and suffocating space. I was fifty-five when that memory surfaced. I cried. I had never attached those words to my mother.

I learned to go through my black holes. The first one was the hardest. It's a *Twilight Zone* moment not knowing what to expect or what was going to happen. I was scared, but I had to learn to let go. Soon I recognized the wave of sadness that appeared, and I allowed myself to go through my black hole. I saw snippets of my past clearly. I saw myself as a little girl and I understood my fear and pain and what I endured. I was overwhelmed with pride for that little girl. Peace flooded my being and I became stronger. On the other side of the black hole was healing. Not only did I learn to go through my black holes, I welcomed them.

I had to allow the pain to surface so I could heal from it. Forty-five years of hiding from emotional pain and abuses. Now I was willing to face it all to obtain a quality life. For the first time I cried about the loss of my marriage to Jesse eighteen years earlier.

Repressed memories often surface during middle age because we are many years removed from the abuse, we are more in control of our life, and we are in a better place. My mind kept the bad memories hidden and protected me until it knew I was in a good place and able to deal with my past.

Prior to my repressed memories surfacing, I had a nice weekly routine with my husband, daughter, and father. I enjoyed my social life with friends at the marina and I loved being on the water. My life was happy and I was in a good place.

Before the repressed memories surfaced at age forty-five, I knew my parents fought a lot and drank too much, but I wasn't aware of how sick they were until those childhood memories surfaced. With each new memory, I was given a new piece of the puzzle and I started to come out of hiding.

31

The IT Guy

I COMPLETED INDIVIDUAL AND GROUP THERAPY after three and a half years. The next four years I enjoyed taking writing classes at the Loft in Minneapolis and meeting with my writer's group once a month. I did some dating and didn't marry anyone. It was good to live closer to Sarah again. She was still in her apartment on the sixth floor in St. Paul. I moved to Minneapolis to be near my work, the Loft and my writer's group.

One day while I was at work, Doug, a co-worker, came into the office and asked, "Dody, are you seeing anyone."

"Doug, that's a strange question. Aren't you married?"

"No, I mean, yes, I am. I'm not asking for me. I have a good friend who's single. He's real nice and owns his own computer business. I think you two should meet."

"I'm sure your friend is very nice, but I'm taking a break from dating right now. But thanks for thinking of me."

Two weeks later my computer crashed and I asked Doug if his friend would look at it. He called Lyle on the spot. Doug instructed me, "Bring your CPU to work tomorrow, and I'll take it to Lyle. He said he'll fix it for a nice dinner."

"Thanks!"

Lyle called a few times during the week with computer questions and then to say my computer was ready. He arrived at five o'clock on Saturday and, after my computer was up and running, we walked to Duigi's, an Italian restaurant not far from my apartment. I liked him. He was easy to be with. On our second date we went to pick up a canoe he purchased and went out to dinner again. We dated for a year doing fun things like canoeing, hiking and visiting the north shore a few times. I love Lake Superior and walking on the breaker wall in Grand Marais.

We were married a year after we met in the back yard of Lyle's home. He had lived there twenty-five years and now it was my home. I met most of Lyle's family at our wedding from both his mother and father's side. It was easy to fall in love with his family and their affection for me was returned.

I spent most of my life looking for that magical family that Artie and I dreamed about and when I stopped looking, it showed up at my front door holding a computer. Lyle was my first husband after my childhood memories surfaced and after I did the hard work in therapy.

The other day I was thinking back to the time when we met, and I said to him, "I can't believe you fixed my computer for the price of a dinner."

"Yeah, but I got a nice wife out of it."

32

Mom Called

ABOUT SIX MONTHS INTO THERAPY after my repressed memories surfaced, I was told my healing would not be hampered if my father was in my life. But, if I wanted to move forward in my healing and work towards a strong healthy life, I would have to end the relationship with my mother.

Soon after I was given that information, my mother called to say she was upset with one of her kids. She was always mad at one of us. She changed all the time who wasn't allowed at her funeral if she were to die that week.

I said to her, "Mom, I can't do this anymore."

"Do what?"

"I can't have these conversations. I don't want to hear who you're angry at. I'm trying to heal, Mom, and I need to let you go."

"I won't say things that upset you then."

"I love you Mom. I don't blame you. Mom, you too, have had a hard life."

"No, I haven't. Nobody had a better childhood than me. My life has been very good. But, if I can't be in your life anymore than I will respect that."

We hung up and my mother and I didn't talk for twelve years. I've missed her over the years, but my life improved when I eliminated the verbal beatings she inflicted on me or my siblings. In a weakened moment I went to a minister I knew and told him it had been ten years since my mother and I talked. Did he agree with the therapist that in order for me to heal, she couldn't be in my life? I was so hoping he would take the forgiveness road and give me full permission to open the doors of communication with her. He did not. He said, "Sometimes we have to let go of those we love in order to love ourselves and grow into the people we were meant to be. Sometimes we have to let go of a parent to end the abuse in our lives."

Two more years went by and then one day while I was working in my shop, the phone rang.

"Hello, this is Dody."

"Hello, Dody. This is Mom."

I didn't think I heard right, "Who is this?"

"This is your mom."

At first I thought it was someone playing a joke on me. I didn't recognize the voice."

"Who is this?"

"It's Mom, your mother."

"Mom, how are you?"

"I'm good. How are you?"

"Good."

"I know you're busy. I better let you get back to work. I love you, Dody."

"I love you too, Mom."

It was a strange conversation for a mother and daughter to have who hadn't talked to each other in twelve years. It must have been very hard for her to make that call. I was pleased that my mother called me that day and I thought, *I can do this. She's eighty-two years old and she's not going to be around much longer.*

A few days later, I was gone all day when she left a message on my answering machine.

"Hi, Dody, this is Mom. I was just listening to Susan Boyle and it made me think of you." Later in the day she left another message.

"Hi, Dody, it's Mom again. It sounds like you have a cold, or maybe it's just your sexy voice I hear?" I didn't get home until late so I called her the next day.

"Hi, Mom. I was gone all day yesterday."

"You must be very busy. I'm worried that you have a cold."

"No, I don't have a cold."

"Have you heard of Susan Boyle? She sings so beautifully."

"Yes I have. I love listening to her and she's so adorable. Wouldn't it be fun to spend an afternoon with her?"

"I know you're very busy. I better let you get back to work. I love you, Dody. Bye."

"I love you too, Mom."

Anger visited me that day. She traveled throughout my bloodstream, consuming every inch of me. Instead of throwing something, I cried out loud, "*You ended my marriage. You told my husband I was cheating on him. I forgive you, but I will never trust you.*" I sent this letter to my mother.

February 14th, 2010

Dear Mom,

I love you tremendously and I think of the good memories I have with you and there are many.

Mom, you're the funniest person I know and I loved your humor.

I loved the time you and Kathy and I went to a Christian Woman's Retreat together for a weekend. We enjoyed good food and listened to great speakers and we laughed our heads off in our room at night.

I loved it when Kathy drove down from Rochester and the three of us stayed up all night talking.

I loved our years of playing Bingo together.

I think of the good stuff, Mom.

Today, I'm very happy and I've healed a lot, but talking to you takes me back to times when it wasn't good. I wish I could shut off that part of my brain. It's been twelve years since we've talked and I thought I could do it, but I can't. Again, I need to let you go because the bad stuff comes up again after we talk. I wish it didn't, but it does.

You are loved by ALL your children, Mom, and I know one thing for certain, you did the best you could with what you had raising us. I don't blame you or feel anger towards you.

Mom, I love Sarah more than life itself, but she too needs to heal from her childhood and find the strong woman and spirit inside of her. I meant her no harm and only wanted a good life for her, but that didn't happen. I don't blame myself, because I know I did the best I could with what I had, just like you did. But, sometimes people get hurt and I have to let Sarah do what ever she has to do to heal and grow.

I'm sorry, Mom, I wish it didn't have to be like this. But, after we talk, the memories come back and I hurt more.

Love,

Dody

My mother could barely see so my sister Kathy read the letter to her. Kathy called me the next day to tell me Mom thought the letter was wonderful and she understood.

"Dody, as soon as I finished reading it, Mom said, 'I must call her and tell her it's okay, I understand.' I had to explain to her that probably wasn't a good idea and a letter might be nice. Mom is sending you a letter."

"That's a great idea. I might be able to do letters. We can try that at least."

A few days later I received this letter from my mother.

Dear Dody,

So happy to read your letter, and I love you very much. I'm happy that you're healing. You're a good mother and did the best you could. Sarah is very lucky to have you as her mom.

Kathy read your letter to me, and my friend Dolly is writing this for me.

Kathy and I remembered all our trips to the taco restaurant with you and Sarah. Those were fun times.

I'm always praying for you and your family.

Love,

Mom

February 26, 2010

Dear Mom,

I received your letter today. Thank you for your kind words. I love our writing to each other. It feels special. Now we can talk comfortably without feeling hurried because one of us has to do something.

My husband, Lyle, and I live in the country complete with dirt road. We have a small lake in the back yard and woods on both sides of our house. We actually live in Lent Township, and Lyle has been a supervisor on the board for the past twelve years. I join him at our monthly township meetings, township supervisors meetings, county commissioners meetings, township staff meetings and social engagements that come up. In September he was chosen to go to Washington for a week to represent townships in our county and I went with him. We stayed at a bed & breakfast in an old brownstone building. I wrote during the day while he attended meetings and every night we walked around Washington and found a neighborhood restaurant to eat at.

Lyle is self-employed with his computer business, and I'm self-employed with my furniture and decorating business. Besides politics and work I belong to a writer's group. We meet once a month to help each other with writing projects. I write stories about my life and I'm sending you two that are fun. "A six-year-old business" about Artie and me selling candy in the neighborhood in Garden City. It's funny because today my business is selling used treasures I find. The other story is "Rearranging the Neighborhood" about the time I totally decorated the Spear's home across the street from us in East Northport. I hope you enjoy them.

I joined Toastmasters in December to overcome my fear of talking in front of people. All of my adult life whenever I needed to pull a happy thought out because something stressful just happened, I would say to myself, "Thank God, I don't belong to Toastmasters." But I love it. I entered our club's contest and won. Last night was the next level of competition for our district and I came in first place. I received a trophy and certificate. Whoever would have thought my first trophy would come from Toast-masters? The next level of competition is the Prairie Division Contest on Saturday, March 13th. Last night after the competition, many people came up to me and told me how funny I was. I'm sure I get that from you.

God is still number one in my life and I talk with him daily. I believe he guides me on the path I should take and opens the doors I should walk through and I thank him for the doors he closes. I'm thankful that you and I are communicating.

Please tell me how you spend your days. It must be nice to have Bill, Bob, and Kathy nearby. Tell me about your church. Delma sounds like a good friend. Since it's hard to see, do you listen to books in a recorder? I would love to hear about you.

Do you remember your Duluth winters growing up? After the first snow which often comes in November the ground turns white and stays until March or April. It took me years to get used to that. Now I know I'm a true Minnesotan because it's a warm day if we hit thirty. It was minus six when we woke up this morning. March is my favorite month because I know winter is leaving and spring is arriving.

I love you, Mom, and look forward to your next letter,
Dody

33

My Parents' Story

EVERY SO OFTEN MY DAD TOLD THE STORY about how his father died. He began with, "My father traveled a lot and was a sleepwalker. He always moved a dresser or large piece of furniture in front of the window when he traveled, fearful that he may walk out the window in the middle of the night while sound asleep." Dad continued with his story. "My father was on a business trip when I was nine years old. He arrived at the hotel exhausted from a full day of travel and meeting with clients. He stopped in the lounge for a nightcap before retiring to bed. In the middle of the night, still asleep, he walked out of his hotel window and fell to his death. He forgot to move a large item in front of the window."

I came across a *Chicago Tribune* newspaper when I was cleaning out my dad's apartment. The words on the front page read, "Steel Tycoon dies at home from sleepwalking," and there was a picture of Grandpa White.

I read the story in the paper which was quite different from my dad's version. The paper stated, "Arthur S. White was at home with his family when in the middle of the night he was sleepwalking and walked out their second-story bedroom window to his death when he hit the cement driveway below. He leaves

156

behind his wife, Willa, his son, Arthur, age five, and daughter, Jody, age six."

I wondered why Dad didn't tell the story like the newspaper. Why did he tell me he was nine when he was actually five? Why did he say his dad was away when it was at home where he died? I'm a sleepwalker myself and I was told a sleepwalker never puts him or herself in harm's way when sleepwalking. I'm not sure I believe the article in the paper. I can only speculate that I think it was an accident at home. What ever happened that evening, I'm sure it was confusing for a little boy.

My dad's mother married again and her second husband drowned when he fell out of the boat they were in. She married a third time and had that marriage annulled because she feared he would die also. All I know of my father's childhood is that the family moved a lot and he spent many years in boarding schools.

I don't know much about my mother's childhood either. She was the third child born and the only daughter. She had two older brothers and a younger one. My mother told this story about her childhood. "When I was thirteen years old my older brother Frank came home from school and lay down on the sofa saying he didn't feel well. He died in his sleep that day at the age of seventeen. Soon after the death of her brother, her other older brother who was studying to be a priest was diagnosed with schizophrenia and institutionalized when he was in his twenties. My mother lost her two older brothers in a short period of time and I sensed that she also lost both her parents emotionally at her young age. I don't know much about her father, but I do know her mother went to church every day from the day her son died until the day she died of old age.

At the age of eighty-two my mother told my sister the real story, a secret she'd kept for sixty-nine years. She began, "I was thirteen years old when my father and my brother Frank were fighting. Dad had just learned from his son's girlfriend's father that

157

she was pregnant. My brother and father fought with their fists at the top of the stairs when my brother fell down the full flight. He was taken to the hospital and died the next day. The family never spoke of this to anyone. My parents stopped speaking all together. I tried to talk my mother into getting help but no one would listen to me."

It's obvious my parents were both wounded before they married each other and started their own family. I have no doubt that they came from abusive, violent backgrounds. I don't believe their rage, violence, alcoholism, and depression came out of nowhere, it came from somewhere.

In the 1920s there wasn't much available for treatment of depression or mental illness. There was no escape for the children who were born into unhealthy environments and not much help for the parents. What people did behind closed doors was their business and you could pretty much do whatever you wanted to your spouse and children.

I learned a lot about abuse, pain, loss, and surviving in therapy. I learned how our brain protects us from acts of violence and trauma. I understand why we try to hide from the pain with alcohol, drugs, sex, and work—just about anything can help diminish the pain. I believe my parents' pain was deep and they refused to let it surface. How could they? Who would help them if it did?

Every time my mother gave birth, she blocked out the childbirth experience and denied that it happened. During that time you wouldn't think there was anything wrong with her except that she didn't recognize she just had a baby. Dad loved to tell the story about people coming over to the house to see the new baby and Mom saying, "What baby?" and everyone laughing.

After Kathy, Artie, and I were born, a woman came to live with us until Mom was aware that she had a baby and started caring for her child. When Billy and Bobby were born, Kathy took care of them. She was ten when Bill was born and twelve when Bob came along.

I love both my parents more than anyone can imagine. Partly because I believe they came from a place similar to mine. I was able to forgive them because in my surviving life and doing the best I could with what I had, bestowed onto my daughter a childhood filled with pain and loss that she will have to heal from.

34

If You Divorce This One, Mom, I'm Marrying Him

THREE YEARS AFTER LYLE AND I MARRIED we started talking to Sarah about moving in with us. We watched her become more depressed each day and her struggles to accomplish the simplest tasks like washing her dishes, taking a shower or going to the grocery store was almost impossible. She was in a severe depression and crying every day. I was afraid if she went any lower she wouldn't be with us much longer.

The day came when Sarah called me, "Mom, I don't want to quit my job and I don't want to lose my apartment, but I can't even leave this stinking place. Will you help me?" We moved Sarah and her cat, Raymus, into our home. She slept for the first few weeks. I had no idea how hard life was for her. My girl lived everyday with anxiety and panic attacks. She obsessed and worried about everything and she suffered from extreme low self-esteem. She was thirty-two and broken.

My heart ached for her. Having Sarah under my roof again, I thought about the day she was born and our first stay in the hospital. It was 9:30 on a Sunday morning when I woke up to take a shower before church. I was nine months pregnant. I stepped into the tub and my water broke. I thought, *How convenient*. I stepped out, dried off and went into the bedroom to wake Jesse up. "Honey, my water just broke while I was taking a shower. I'll call Dr. Hu and find out what to do."

"What did the doctor say?"

"She said, the contractions should start soon and call her when they're ten minutes apart and then leave for the hospital."

The contractions were ten minutes apart at noon. I called Dr. Hu and we left to go have a baby. *Soon I'll be holding my daughter or son.* At 1:00 in the afternoon, I was moved into the delivery room and Sarah was born a half hour later at 1:32.

The doctor took Sarah and placed her into Jesse's arms. After a few moments a nurse took Sarah from Jesse and said, "We have to bathe her now." I wanted to ask to see her, but I didn't. Friends and family started arriving in my room after viewing our little girl. Everyone told me how pretty she was and I believed them. I still didn't know why they weren't bringing her to me. I fell asleep with my tears that night thinking, *It's not supposed to be like this.* Monday, I received more visitors and I listened closely to what they said trying to find a clue as to why my daughter wasn't with me. I still heard how beautiful she was, but did she have all her toes? They didn't know because she was covered up. I was sad because everyone saw my daughter but me and I hid my feelings well.

Tuesday came and went and I still hadn't seen my baby.

Wednesday morning arrived, the day I was to leave the hospital with my daughter. My mother-in-law, Paula, walked into the room exuberantly and said, "How are mother and daughter today?"

I told her, "I'm fine, but I haven't seen Sarah yet."

"You haven't seen her? Good. Maybe I'll catch her with you this morning. You'll be leaving to go home in a few hours."

"No, I've never seen her."

"What?"

It all gushed out of me as I cried, "I've never seen Sarah, and I'm scared to death something is wrong with her and they don't know how to tell me."

"There is nothing wrong with your daughter. She is perfect."

Paula was a registered nurse at the hospital and as she ran out of my room I could hear her yelling in the hall for Nurse Pine. Within five minutes Paula came back holding Sarah and placed her in my arms. She was a beautiful baby and I never wanted to let go of her. Paula left the room and quietly closed the door behind her.

After I checked all her beautiful little fingers and toes, I said, "Hi, honey. I'm your mom. I waited five years, nine months and two weeks for you to join your father and me. I'm sorry it took three days for us to meet. I want for you, Sarah, to have a wonderful life full of love and happiness. Your father loves you and I love you and you will always be safe. You're going to grow up in a beautiful home in the best little village in the world. You have a great grandmother and grandma and grandpa that live in that village. Besides me, there are so many people happy you were born. I love you." I hugged my little girl close to my heart.

Jesse picked us up at the hospital. Holding my daughter we drove home with Shame, my newly found acquaintance that became a fixture of who I was. I was convinced now as if I needed convincing that something was seriously wrong with me. I hated the mother who couldn't ask to see her own baby. Little did I know, that would be only the first time I wouldn't be there for my daughter. Self-hate secretly grew inside of me. I believe this was why I worked hard on my talents. Something had to compensate for not being a good mother.

I cried every time I thought of the time Sarah was born. She deserved so much more. I wanted her to have a life that she felt safe in and received love, support and praise. Instead, she got me.

I looked at Sarah, now weak and frail at thirty-two, and I thought to myself, *She is the strongest person I know for surviving the childhood handed to her.* Who was there for her when we moved away from her dad, grandparents, GG, and Cattaraugus? Who was there for her when we moved away from Jason and the boys? Who

162

helped her the year we moved to Minnesota? I was fortunate. I lost years of my childhood even as they were happening. Unfortunately for Sarah, she was always aware of hers, and there was no escaping the pain.

Throughout Sarah's growing up years every person and thing that she loved and cared about was taken from her.

Sarah's survival was to not allow anything or anyone into her life that she might care about. How could she let something good enter her world when eventually it would disappear? Sarah's life was void of hope, trust, believing in anything, including herself.

When I was growing up, no matter what was happening, I had Artie, and I had years with the same friends and attending the same school. Kathy, Bill, and Bob were constant in my life. Who was constant in Sarah's life?

Sarah asked me the other day, "How come you're so good to me? A lot of parents would have given up on their kid."

"Honey, I worked hard to get to this place. You deserve to have good."

"I'm going to work hard also."

I'm fortunate to be present in my daughter's life today. I mean that twofold, I'm present and not blocking out time and I don't take for granted her allowing me to be in her life. I'm the very source and the root for her heartaches and losses. Today I have this opportunity to give her what she needs most from me—support her life.

Sarah and I went for a walk one day about six months after she moved in and she said, "You know why I hate the mornings?"

"No, why?"

"Because they smell like school." That was the first thing she told her therapist.

Lyle is a strong, loving step-dad. He's a good male role model for Sarah and he's the first man in her life she has received unconditional love and support from. On one of our walks she said, "If you divorce this one, Mom, I'm marrying him."

Sarah came to live with Lyle and me and started the hard work of healing. She moved into her own apartment a year later. I will always be amazed by her strength and soon she will learn of the stuff she is made of and will amaze herself. She lives nearby and we see each other often.

35

Free and Clear

ARAH AND I VISITED CATTARAUGUS twenty-one years after I left. I longed to touch and breathe the most wonderful place in the world. A part of my healing was to go back and face my painful losses: where my first marriage and Sarah's birth took place, my first home, my best friend Lynn, my new family John, Paula and GG, and the place where I found God.

When we first arrived, I wished I had never left. I overwhelmed myself with questions of why I had. Why didn't I find an apartment in Cattaraugus when Sarah's father and I separated? Why didn't I raise her in this wonderful village surrounded by family and friends and consistency? I had to stop tormenting myself with questions and accept that I did the best I could with what I had.

The first day Sarah and I arrived in Cattaraugus, I pulled up in front of the Deli and saw a very thin, old man sweeping the sidewalk a few storefronts away. We stared at each other for a while and then I said, "Calvin?" He said, "Dody?" We held each other in a strong embrace. I knew at that moment he was back with his loving God. There was much healing in that hug and I followed Calvin inside to see Corinth, his storefront church on Main Street. I wasn't sure if anyone was left from the original group. If so, I would guess a handful. It looked like he had a nice congregation.

Lynn's mother was traveling at the time, so Sarah and I had her house to ourselves. Every evening we sat on the back deck overlooking the town and reflected about the day and memories from our past. We spent our afternoons with Lynn playing chauffer driving us to all our requested places. We visited the Amish community just outside of Cattaraugus where I drove when my parents fought on weekend afternoons. I watched barn raisings and purchased pies and breads just so I could enter their calm, simplistic, orderly homes. On this trip I bought hand-woven placemats created on their looms.

I've never had a best friend I've been closer to than Lynn. Although I couldn't relate to her, I observed her strong, self-confident, fearless character. Her mightiness did not rub off on me but she gave me years to reflect about her strength and to wonder how someone obtained that?

I was at my writer's group near the completion of this book when a fellow writer asked, "Are you writing this book for your family?" That question stopped me in my tracks. I immediately thought of my brothers and sister. We grew up learning not to talk to each other. Don't get too close to one another and don't feel anything. I have no idea what their reaction will be when they find out our life growing up has been brought out into the open. *I love you, Kathy, Bill, and Bob, and I wish you no harm. All I want is to continue to love you and for us to talk.* My brothers and sister live near Buffalo, New York.

My sister, Kathy, raised three daughters and a son mostly by herself. She is a devoted, loving mother and grandmother. She has a strong faith in God.

My brother Bill works full time in a printing shop and lives with his three cats. He is the most sensitive and tender hearted of all of us. He is content and at peace with the quiet tranquil life he has carved out for himself.

My brother Bob, his wife, Mary Ann, and their daughter, Erika, live in Hamburg a few blocks from Lake Erie. Bob is a

Professional Christian Clown and aspires to be a missionary or Christian comedian. Either way he will bring happiness into people's lives as he does now. His natural wit and good humor flows out of him with every sentence. It's obvious he loves to make people laugh.

Bess, Artie's wife, has remained a close sister. It was easy to connect with Bess because we both loved Artie and maybe because we didn't share a family history of negative conditioning. She is my rock. Today Bess spends her time with friends, hiking and traveling. She worked many years in Hospice as a caregiver and still lives in the Berkshires.

In my adult life I spent seven years in therapy. It helped me understand my life and guide me towards my new future. I arrived at the place where I said, "Enough therapy. I need to go and live my life and find my own way. I will make mistakes and have to repair bad choices, but I will learn and grow and live my life as best I can. I will never be alone again. My safety nets are in place and I will ask for help if I'm drowning.

I wanted to write this book to bring my life out into the open after having hidden it and been quiet for so many years. A tremendous amount of healing came from writing it.

Going back and reliving my life in chronological order revealed my past to me in a way I've never seen before. By writing I saw my daughter's life and looked at what she had to endure growing up for the first time. For that breakthrough alone, I'm glad I wrote it. Writing a book is like raking the rocks, the more I write, the more there is to write.

There is no cure for growing up in a violent home or being sexually abused as a child. I will continue to heal until the day I die. Everyday it's a little easier to cope with memories that surface, and sometimes I can embrace them. I survived my difficult, wearisome and sometimes life-threatening journey. I did the hard work and today I have a quality life.

Near the end of writing this book the most painful memory of all surfaced and I allowed the pain to take precedence. For two days I saw clearly that losing time was how I survived throughout my life, time I will never get back. In order to have a repressed memory surface, first you have to have a memory. I lived my life repressing memories and living in a fugue state. My repressed memories can surface; the times that I disappeared cannot.

The times that I was in a fugue state are gone and I cried, longing for the missed holidays with Sarah, her birthdays and her first day of school. After two days my tears stopped but the sadness did not. I mourned the loss of my daughter's childhood.

One week after realizing how much time I lost in my life, I woke up early. It was a special day. I had my outfit picked out for weeks. I showered and styled my hair. I was going to look my prettiest today.

I wondered why this day felt more special than any other. *In a few hours I will be presenting my speech at Toastmasters. What's the big deal about that? I've been going to Toastmaster's once a week for five months and this was my fourth speech. Oh, yeah, this will be my first time speaking out loud to a group of people about the violence in my home growing up.*

As I was getting ready I looked down at my cat and said, "Biscuit, I need to soak in a bath this afternoon." My body hurt just like it did when I was eight.

As I drove home that day after giving my speech, I was flying high on top of the world, and I knew my life had just changed again. I didn't know until after I gave my speech that I'd lived everyday with pain. It wasn't until the pain disappeared that I realized it existed. Something I had felt all my life was now gone. I knew this healing was connected to the time in the third grade when I was going to tell the doctor about my parents. When the weekly trips to the doctor ended, so did my window to tell. Giving that speech in Toastmasters was my "telling" and after doing so, forty-nine years of physical pain disappeared.

In therapy we were encouraged to write and publish our story. June said, "Self-publish if you have to. It doesn't matter if anyone ever reads it. You wrote it and you put it out there for the world to see. Your secrets and your past will be in the open and you will be free." I am free and clear.

Today, I enjoy going to my shop and building something from scratch.

Epilogue

I CRINGE WHEN I HEAR THE WORDS, "Scream, kick, run and tell someone when a stranger has grabbed you." Something inside screams back: "Where does the child go when it is home that is hurting her?"

It is good to teach our children to scream, kick, run and tell. They need to be empowered to control their surroundings, but when home is the most dangerous place they know, they will need something far more than a slogan.

Our most vulnerable are still being raped and abused in their homes. Little voices, full of potential and talent, are silenced by parents, relatives, and siblings in a vicious game of hide and seek, catch and release. But it is the victim who doesn't know what to do with a release scarred by memories and feelings that hide like monsters under their beds.

Statistics maintain that one in every four girls is sexually abused before age eighteen, one in six for boys. That means there are thirty-nine million survivors of childhood sexual abuse in America alone. Every year close to three million children are reported harmed and neglected—picture a population the size of Chicago. Every year 1,800 children die from violence and neglect in the United States.

For me it was not finding a safe place that made me close in on myself. I grew up feeling unloved and damaged. My low self-esteem made it a huge challenge just to survive each day, and the nights brought their own terrors. My escape was to make the monsters disappear by forgetting.

Our boys and girls need to know there are safe places to run, to find help. The story of my life shows where to find that place. They need to know they are not "damaged goods," and they no longer need to believe such lies. They can draw from the inner strength that helped them survive childhood horrors and begin the process of healing. The earlier that abused and neglected children get help, the greater chance they have to move forward towards the quality life they were meant to have.

I will speak out to help stop violence in our homes until our children feel safe. It is the law to report suspected child abuse 1-800-422-4453.

The statistics are one in every four girls and one in every six boys is sexually abused. The numbers have not changed in the last fifty years since I was a child because ninety percent of child molesters target their own children or children they know well and eighty-eight percent of children who are molested by someone they know don't tell. If we educate our children about sexual abuse from pre-kinder-garten through fifty grade we will lower the numbers significantly because in eighty percent of the cases of children who are sexually abused, molestation starts at the age of eight or older.

Most importantly, by educating children about sexual abuse, how many of them will be spared later in life from a prison sentence, drug and alcohol addictions, medical conditions as a result of their childhood molestation, from years of therapy, and the list goes on.

Let's encourage the prevention of child sexual abuse by asking for speakers to come to our churches, our clubs, organizations, whenever we gather to break the silence. We know from the testimonies both from victims and perpetrators that SILENCE makes abuse possible.